TRUTH AND CONSEQUENCES

TRUTH AND CONSEQUENCES:
THE QUIZ SHOW SCANDALS OF THE 1950s AND THEIR AFTERMATH

DAVID INMAN

BearManor Media

2025

Published in the United States of America by:

BearManor Media

1317 Edgewater Dr. #110
Orlando, FL 32804

bearmanormedia.com

Printed in the United States.

Typesetting and layout by PKJ Passion Global

ISBN–979-8-88771-703-6

To Joyce — Again and Always.

CONTENTS

PREFACE

"No matter how cynical you get, it's never enough to keep up."
— *Lily Tomlin in* The Search for Signs of Intelligent Life in
the Universe, *written by Jane Wagner*

The 1950s are often referred to as the golden age of American television drama, and during that era programs such as *Playhouse 90, Kraft Television Theatre* and *U.S. Steel Hour* certainly presented memorable plays and performances.

But the biggest television drama of the 1950s wasn't a romance, or a western, or a cop show.

It was a real-life morality play — one about greed, about fraud, and about cheating, about shame and dishonor. It began in a producer's study on Park Avenue, led to hit shows on two television networks, then to a Manhattan grand jury, and finally a congressional hearing room in Washington. As it unfolded careers were wrecked, reputations were ruined and a monolithic form of broadcast advertising that had dominated for decades finally came crashing down.

It was the TV quiz-show scandals of the late 1950s — deception on a grand scale that played out on a small screen. Three shows in particular — *The $64,000 Question, The $64,000 Challenge,* and *Twenty-One* — were the worst offenders and, for a time, the most popular TV programs in the country.

After those shows skyrocketed in popularity and some contestants became beloved celebrities, the nation learned that all was not as it seemed — that many of the contestants went on the air already knowing the questions they would be asked as well as the answers to those questions, as well as how to "perform" when answering them on the air for maximum dramatic effect.

Hundreds of thousands of dollars were given to quiz winners as Americans sat on the edges of their Barcaloungers, thinking everything they saw was spontaneous, above board and proof of the American dream — that hard work, dedication and study could pay off in big bucks and Cadillac convertibles (the consolation prize on *The $64,000 Question*). The shows were more than entertainment — they were a sort of tribal ritual that drew millions to their televisions each week to see if last week's winners would leave with the money they had won to that point or whether they would stay and try to win more. And the audience celebrated those wins as a kind of validation of American exceptionalism.

In our more cynical age, we assume that much of what we see on television has been manipulated in some way. We take it with a grain of salt because the tube has tricked us before — many times.

But in the 1950s, when television was still relatively young, there existed an unspoken trust between viewers and what they saw on that new box in the living room. There had never before been a reason to question that trust. The quiz show scandals were a massive, traumatic violation of that trust, and as a result our view of the new medium — and, by extension, of our society at large — began to change.

INTRODUCTION

It is Tuesday, June 7, 1955, ten years after the end of World War II, and America is in the throes of a midcentury love affair with itself.

That day, the government announces that employment is at an all-time high, and so is factory production. The U.S. is at peace, if you don't count the cold war. Just about two months earlier, on April 12, Dr. Jonas Salk's polio vaccine is declared a success after a clinical trial, a milestone celebrated by the ringing of church bells across the country. Salk chooses to make the vaccine accessible to all, forgoing any personal wealth from his discovery.

Everything seems positive and prosperous. Cultural, racial and political upheaval are on vacation. Elvis Presley and rock and roll are in the future. The Rev. Dr. Martin Luther King Jr. and the fight for civil rights are in the future. Vietnam and the twilight of American military dominance are in the future.

It is a time of a booming birthrate, of suburban supremacy, of consumer complacency, and of television takeover. The number of American homes with TV will rise from 20 percent in 1950 to nearly 90 percent in 1960.[1]

On primetime television that June 7, Martha Raye is mugging through her last NBC variety show of the season, with guest Errol Flynn. On the CBS news program *See It Now*, Edward R. Murrow is reporting on the recently discovered link between cigarettes and lung cancer. Within ten years, Murrow, who always cradles a lit cigarette in his hand while visiting celebrities on the interview show *Person to Person*, will himself be dead of the disease.

At 9:30 p.m. eastern time on CBS television, just before *See It Now*, comes a new show, replacing the anthology series *Danger*.

It is a quiz show called *The $64,000 Question*, and nothing quite like it has ever been seen on TV before.

In the center of the stage stands a glassed-in isolation booth. On top is the sponsor's name: REVLON. Flanking the booth's front window are two larger-than-life lipsticks, looking like sleek, red-tipped bullets. Contestants vying for large cash prizes by answering complex questions step into the booth so that they will be isolated from any answers accidentally blurted by someone in the audience — and because it adds to the "plot." For although *The $64,000 Question* is a quiz show, make no mistake — it is paced, planned, and cast like a drama.

Adding to the scene, off to one side, is a new IBM computer that will "scientifically" sort out questions for panelists. The machine is just about as large as the Cadillac convertibles the show gives away as consolation prizes.

On the other side of the stage sits Ben Feit, a vice-president from Manufacturer's Trust Company of New York. On each side of Feit is a uniformed guard. On the table in front of Feit sits a box that has been locked in a safe — a box containing additional quiz questions.

Even the show's emcee is different: Hal March is better known as a light comic actor with a long, but not exactly distinguished, career in TV, with one exception — while appearing with Jackie Gleason on *Cavalcade of Stars* in the early 1950s, Gleason broke March's nose in a fight scene on live TV.[2]

Hal March, best known as a light comic actor,
becomes a star as the low-key emcee of *The $64,000 Question*.

Unlike the average hyperkinetic TV emcee, March is a low-key charmer who chats amiably with contestants, putting them — and the audience — at ease. He's chosen because he won't try to overwhelm the proceedings.

Not that anyone could — the proceedings are overwhelming enough in themselves.

"Ladies and gentlemen," March says, "Revlon welcomes you to a new program with a format that we believe you will find very exciting indeed. On *The $64,000 Question* our contestants will choose categories with which they are familiar. We will ask them specially prepared questions in that category — questions that, for fairness' sake, will be shuffled by our IBM machine here. With each correct answer, a contestant may double his or her winnings, until they reach the final plateau of $64,000!"

"And now," adds March, turning to Revlon commercial spokeswoman Wendy Barrie, "here's Wendy to tell you gals how to put an end to fading lips."[3]

The audience applauds — they applauded the commercials in those days. And throughout America — an America before air-conditioning, an America of front porches and window fans and cold baths taken to break the summer heat — more and more people begin coming in from their porches and sitting in front of their hot TV sets.

CHAPTER ONE: A SHORT HISTORY OF COMMERCIAL BROADCASTING — OR, THE SPONSOR, THE SPOT AND THE STUTTERING SHOWGIRL

"Radio and TV advertising is not a luxury but a necessity . . . a part of everyday living in the United States. Children quote singing commercials as often as they recite nursery rhymes. . . . The sponsor whose bankroll provides information and entertainment is . . . the friend who provides them with temporary escape from their problems. This great public benefactor . . . is providing entertainment and up-to-the-second news . . . . It's nice to know the name of this great guy." -- ad agency time buyer Charlotte Armstrong in Sponsor *magazine, 1950*[1]

By the time *The $64,000 Question* hits the airwaves in 1955, the advertiser has almost monolithic control over television programming and, by extension, the networks themselves. It is the peak of power for the advertiser, the last gasp of a sponsor-dominated model of corporate broadcasting sponsorship that has been in place for over thirty years.

It begins on August 28, 1922, at the dawn of American radio's domination as a mass communication medium. The first commercial announcement over the air is a 10-minute talk on New York station WEAF extolling the virtues of living in a Long Island housing complex. Cost of the commercial: $50. Sales result: $127,000.[2]

Despite that success, advertising on the radio is at first considered a bit, um, gauche. The combination of selling and entertainment is still associated with the common traveling peddler or medicine show barker. Advertising is for billboards, or magazines.

Even Herbert Hoover, then the U.S. Secretary of Commerce, agrees — "[T]he quickest way to kill broadcasting would be to use it for direct advertising," he proclaims.[3]

The powers behind two powerful entities — advertising agencies and broadcast networks — disagree. They sense the potential for a new financial windfall. So whenever the argument is made that radio broadcasting should be commercial-free and financed with a taxed license system, such as the one that funds the British Broadcasting Company, the response is like this, from an article in *Radio Stars* magazine:

"What sort of entertainment do critics of the present system expect from their own Uptopian [sic] scheme? Will they still have [Eddie] Cantor and [Ed] Wynn and the cream of the entire entertainment world night after night after night? Most certainly, they will not! Why? Because no government subsidy would pay Ed Wynn the $5,000 he demands for a performance. No government could afford to present such programs.

"But the advertiser is forced to it by the fact that his advertising is only as effective as his audience is large. So he hunts and invents and devises new and better things to attract listeners. His time on the air costs hundreds of dollars a minute, and he dares not spoil it with mediocre talent. When he fails, he tosses away a fortune. Accordingly, the best brains he can bring to the problem are employed. And the result though not always a happy one is our present self-supporting uncensored style of radio entertainment."[4]

In 1923 comes the first fully-sponsored radio program, featuring the Browning King Orchestra. Browning King is a clothing retailer, and there is no formal commercial during the show — just prominent mention of the orchestra name in between numbers.[5]

The first nationwide radio network, NBC, is launched in 1926, and by now more and more sponsors are buying blocks of time, producing content to fill that time on the schedule and inserting themselves into program titles — *The General Motors Family Party,*

The A&P [grocery chain] Gypsies, The Ipana [toothpaste] Troubadours, The Eveready [battery] Hour.

And radio advertising becomes big business very quickly. Total advertising expenditures in 1929 top $3 billion, of which $20 million is channeled into radio.[6]

A few examples of the power of on-air advertising:

In 1929, vaudeville and stage legend Ed Wynn comes to radio in a program sponsored by Texaco. He portrays a character named the Chief, and he wears a fire chief's hat on the air to plug the sponsor's gasoline. One night, Texaco commercial announcer Graham MacNamee tells listeners that if they fill up with Fire Chief gasoline, they will receive a replica of Wynn's hat. Texaco orders a million hats for the promotion, and ends up ordering two million more to meet demand.

At about the same time, Freeman Gosden and Charles Correll, better known to radio audiences as Amos 'n Andy, begin a promotion for their sponsor, Pepsodent toothpaste. Listeners are told to send in two empty Pepsodent cartons in order to receive a free sample of mouthwash. Two million cartons come pouring in, representing $500,000 in sales (almost $9 million in 2023 dollars).[7]

While the nation is rocked by the Great Depression, radio prospers — both NBC and CBS end the bleak year of 1932 in the black with profits of over a million dollars each.[8]

By the 1930s, commercial broadcasting is in full bloom, and one entity is fully in charge — not the network, but the sponsor. The sponsor hires the advertising agency, which in turn packages and produces the program. Acting on behalf of the sponsor, the agency buys a timeslot (usually ranging from 15 minutes to an hour) on the network schedule, decides what the format will be, who the stars will be, who will supply the music, and who will write, direct and produce the show.

"As the networks saw it," says broadcast historian Eric Barnouw, "this was a perfectly natural thing to do. This was the concept of the network as a phone booth — you buy time and do what you want with it. The networks weren't responsible for what went on, any more than the phone company was responsible for what was said over the telephone."[9]

Sponsors exert control over their programs by inserting as many commercials as the law allows — usually at the beginning, middle and end of the show. They also begin targeting specific audiences who might become customers. During the weekday, daily dramatic serials are fashioned for the housewife and sponsored by household cleaning products like Procter & Gamble's Ivory or Lever Brothers' Lux flakes, leading to the coinage of the phrase "soap opera." On the weekends, broadcast sporting events are sponsored by products aimed at men — cigarettes, pipe tobacco, razor blades, beer, automobiles.

To take advantage of the weekend as the traditional time to go to market, NBC's Thursday night lineup for much of the 1930s is sponsored by food companies — Rudy Vallee's variety hour by Royal Gelatin and Fleischmann's Yeast; *The Maxwell House Showboat*, sponsored by General Foods; and the *Kraft Music Hall*, sponsored by the cheese and dairy goods company.

Some advertisers form long-term relationships with the performers they sponsor — Jack Benny and Jell-O, Johnson's Wax with *Fibber McGee and Molly*, Bing Crosby and Kraft.

A few shows, Benny's *Jell-O Program* especially, feature commercials that are wittily (or at least cleverly) integrated into the program. Benny's contract with sponsors stipulates that his writers, utilizing talking points provided by the ad agency, will write the spots. This leads to commercials like this, from 1936, involving Benny, sidekick Mary Livingstone and announcer Don Wilson:

Jack (to bandleader Johnny Green): "Well anyway, spring is here, so Johnny, play something. You know, something appropriate, like April Showers bring May flowers."

Mary: "And Mayflowers bring pilgrims."

Jack: "And pilgrims bring progress."

Don: "And progress brings Jell-O, with its six delicious flavors: Strawberry, Raspberry, Cherry, Orange, Lemon and Lime!"[10]

Or this, from an episode when Jack exits to call his girlfriend:

Don: "While Jack is making a secret phone call to Lucybelle, let me divert your attention to Jell-O. Jell-O is just as sweet and tempting as Lucybelle and you don't have to be in a phone booth to enjoy it. So remember, always dial J-E-L-L-O, and if the LIME is busy, you can still get strawberry, raspberry, cherry, orange or lemon. Goodbye!"[11] The spots with the light sell fail to impress at least three of Benny's early sponsors — Canada Dry, General Tire and Chevrolet. The powers that be at Canada Dry, in particular, are upset when Benny makes jokes like the one about a girl whose father "drank everything in the United States and then went up north to drink Canada Dry."[12]

Officials at General Foods, the makers of Jell-O, are also so-so about the humorous touch Benny brings to their commercials — until long-dormant sales numbers begin to rise. The integrated comic spots then become a Benny trademark and continue with his subsequent long-time sponsor, Lucky Strike cigarettes.

Benny's creative approach is the exception, however. For the most part, advertisers want their commercials played straight regardless of how obnoxious and patronizing they might be, and performers go along, preferring steady paychecks over principled protests.

Most of the time.

On the other hand, there is the notorious example of the 1942-43 feud between Dan Golenpaul, producer of a radio show called *Information Please*, and the American Tobacco Co., maker of Lucky Strike cigarettes and headed by George Washington Hill.

With the help of public relations expert Edward Bernays, Hill relentlessly builds Lucky Strike into a behemoth brand during the 1920s and early 1930s. Hill and Bernays target the new female smoking audience with the groundbreaking "reach for a Lucky instead of a sweet" campaign. They also coin a well-known catchphrase for Lucky — "It's toasted." The truth is that all cigarettes are made with "toasted" tobacco, but Hill makes it the brand's unique selling point and pounds the phrase into the public consciousness through incessant magazine and radio advertising.

On the radio, Lucky Strike sponsors dance bands in the early 1930s and in 1935 kicks off the long-running *Your Hit Parade*, a weekly roundup of the nation's most popular songs. (One possibly apocryphal story has it that Hill decided what songs to include on *Your Hit Parade* by ordering NBC President Merlin "Deac" Aylesworth to dance with executive Bertha Brainard in order to gauge each number's rhythm possibilities — further demonstrating the power of the sponsor.)[13]

The Lucky Strike radio commercials are an art form in themselves, utilizing tag-team announcers, repeated phrases and a trip-hammer technique that features the fast patter of professional tobacco auctioneers, always ending with the cry "Sold American!" The idea was that American Tobacco, aka Lucky Strike, "consistently select(s) and buy(s) the finer, the lighter, the naturally milder tobacco." This leads to the most famous selling message of all – "LS/MFT," an acronym for "Lucky Strike Means Fine Tobacco" that was tapped out in Morse Code on the radio. There is nothing clever or subtle about the advertising created for Hill by the Lord & Thomas agency — it's all about frequency, repetition and simplicity.

How ironic, then, that a product sold in a way that conveyed an implicit contempt for the intelligence of people ends up sponsoring a show that *celebrates* the intelligence of people.

Because there's Lucky Strike on NBC's *Information Please*, beginning in 1940.

Information Please isn't like anything else on the air. It features four educated and witty panelists answering questions submitted by listeners about practically everything — literature, art, sports, music, movies, science.

The program's creator, Dan Golenpaul, is fanatical about maintaining the qualities that make *Information Please* so unique.

One is a carefully-weighted combination of regular panelists — humorist and columnist Franklin P. Adams, acerbic composer Oscar Levant, Shakespeare expert and sports columnist John Kieran. They're joined each week by a guest from the entertainment, sport, academic or political world — Fred Allen, Boris Karloff, Alfred Hitchcock, composer Deems Taylor, or maybe even New York City mayor Fiorello La Guardia or Republican presidential candidate Wendell Wilkie.

The other special quality is a relaxed, informal atmosphere with brief, dignified commercial interruptions by urbane announcer Milton Cross, best known as the radio voice of the Metropolitan Opera on its Sunday afternoon broadcasts.

Golenpaul understands the financial necessity of commercials, but he believes in keeping them in their place. After Cross completes reading each commercial spot on *Information Please*, moderator Clifton Fadiman unfailingly remarks on the specific number of seconds the spot lasted, as if to reassure the audience that the sponsor isn't running wild and hogging the show.

Unstoppable force Hill and immovable object Golenpaul clash in late 1942, during what are, arguably, the darkest days of World War II.

Hill has decided to redesign the Lucky package, making it white instead of green. What is a purely cosmetic marketing decision is sold as patriotism — the phony explanation is that Lucky Strike is giving up green ink because the military needs it for camouflage.

In classic Hill style, this is turned into an endlessly-repeated phrase that will be drummed into consumers' heads — "Lucky Strike green has gone to war!"[14]

You see it on bus advertisements, in newspapers and magazines, on billboards. And you hear it — over and over and over — on the radio shows Lucky Strike sponsors – *Your Hit Parade*, *Kay Kyser's Kollege of Musical Knowledge*, and *Information Please*.

But you don't hear it as part of a regular commercial — it is literally dropped into the program almost any time there is a pause in the action. So it isn't out of the question to hear something like this:

Cross: Welcome to Information —
Announcer: Lucky Strike green has gone to war!
Cross: — Please.

What might be acceptable on the fast-moving *Your Hit Parade* or on Kay Kyser's freewheeling musical quiz is not accepted on *Information Please*. Because of the show's unique discussion format, witticisms that reward the attentive listener are hidden everywhere. Listening to recordings of the program from that time, you can hear the frustration in moderator Fadiman's voice as the blurted phrase interrupts the rhythm of the show.[15]

Golenpaul is apoplectic, and takes American Tobacco to court. Hill responds with the classic sponsor's viewpoint — since he's paying for *Information Please*, he can do whatever he pleases. But Hill doesn't want negative headlines, so American Tobacco cancels its sponsorship, and *Information Please* quickly finds a new sponsor in the H.J. Heinz Co.[16]

But Hill still has the last word(s) — despite Golenpaul's plea, a judge rules that the final two episodes of *Information Please* sponsored by American Tobacco will have to include Hill's *new* obnoxious phrase, designed to promote the show that Luckies will sponsor instead of *Information Please*. That phrase is "The best tunes of all move to Carnegie Hall" to tease the upcoming *Your All-Time Hit Parade*, which will originate from the famous venue. So, in essence, not only do the panelists on *Information Please* have to put up with

Hill's interjected advertising, but they have to put up with interjected advertising for the show that is replacing them.

Golenpaul argues in court filings that the "Lucky Strike green" phrase as used is "low, vulgar and offensive," and the judge doesn't disagree. "It would undoubtedly have been in much better taste" for American Tobacco to accede to Golenpaul's request, he writes, but he decides it doesn't warrant a court injunction.[17]

***

The growth of advertising agencies parallels the growth in commercial radio broadcasting — in 1938, for the first time, radio passes magazines as a source of advertising revenue.[18]

The next year, 1939, RCA, through its property NBC, begins regular television broadcasting in New York City. And even though commercial advertising is going full bore on radio, the FCC is hesitant to let RCA sell commercial time on the new medium of TV.

But the folks at RCA find a loophole: a sponsor can get a sales message across on TV if it packages and pays for an entire show — the model currently being used in radio. So in the early fall of 1939, Geller's Shoes sponsors George Ross, columnist with the New York *World-Telegram*, in a series of celebrity interviews on NBC. Perhaps "celebrity" is more of an aspirational term — Ross's first guests are yoga expert Tony Soma and Mary Dowell, whose claim to fame is that she is Broadway's tallest showgirl (six foot three inches) and that she stutters.

Variety reviews the first show, and has this to say about the commercial:

"Mildred Murray and Mildred Gale handled the long commercial at the end, after the announcer, Gilbert Martin, had given a name plug earlier. Gals picked up and put down shoes as they pointed out the fine points of each. Difficulty was that the object of attention was too frequently out of range of the camera, so that the shoes couldn't be shown."[19]

(For the record, TV's first official commercial spot is considered a 10-second ad for Bulova watches airing July 1, 1941 on NBC, before a game between the Brooklyn Dodgers and Philadelphia Phillies.)[20]

The development of television is slowed by World War II, but by the late 1940s, network television and radio begin to co-exist and advertising dominates the mediums — and American culture — as never before, both through frequent commercial spots and through best-selling fictional books about the ad game, including *The Hucksters*, *Mr. Blandings Builds His Dream House*, and *The Man in the Gray Flannel Suit*. President Eisenhower's Secretary of Defense, Neil McElroy, comes from an advertising and promotion background at Procter & Gamble, and is dubbed "the first adman cabinet officer."

In 1952, historian David Potter writes: "Advertising now compares with such long-standing institutions as the school and the church in the magnitude of its social influence. It dominates the media, it has vast power in the shaping of popular standards, and it is really one of the very limited group of institutions which exercise social control."[21]

The advertising model that thrived in commercial radio — with sponsors owning blocks of time on the schedule — continues on television into the mid-1960s. Performers, paid by the advertiser, gladly do TV commercials. Sometimes they're even done in character — Andy and Opie Taylor eat Post Toasties corn flakes on *The Andy Griffith Show*, for example, and Fred Flintstone smokes Winston cigarettes. On *The Dick Van Dyke Show*, Rob and Laura Petrie do the dishes with Joy liquid detergent and smoke Kent cigarettes (the show had sponsors that alternated each week). Granny Clampett eats Kellogg's Corn Flakes on *The Beverly Hillbillies* and Jed Clampett joins Flintstone in smoking Winstons (again, alternate weekly sponsors). By the late 1960s, this model fades from popularity as more advertisers abandon buying large blocks of time and turn to an advertising method that promises a more diverse audience — "spot" advertising, peppering individual commercials across a variety of shows rather than spending time and money producing an entire program. This means the sponsor forfeits any direct control over the content of the show — but given the public trauma over the connection between sponsor control and the quiz show scandals, advertisers are just as happy to move on to a new model.

***

But the traditional model — with the sponsor as dominant force — is still the norm in 1955, when the story of *The $64,000 Question* begins with three men:

    * Louis Cowan, a long-time producer and packager of radio and TV shows;

    * Walter Craig, VP of the Norman, Craig & Kummel advertising agency;

    * And last but not least — not by a long shot — Charles Revson, who co-founded Revlon in 1932 and will run the cosmetics firm as president and chairman of the board until his death in 1975.

Cowan: The Brains

Louis George Cowan has a track record of programming successes — his *Quiz Kids* was on radio from 1940-53 and on TV from 1949-53. Cowan is also behind *Stop the Music*, the radio quiz (later on TV as well) that enters the record books because it becomes an instant hit in the late 1940s and helps speed the cancellation of its competitor, a show hosted by legendary comedian Fred Allen.

In August 1955, after *The $64,000 Question* is a hit, Cowan's process of creating the show in his Park Avenue study is elaborately recounted in *The New York Times*:

"He arose one clear morning last January at 7:30, went downstairs to his dining room in pajamas and dressing gown as is his wont, having neither showered nor shaved; ate breakfast (white toast, butter and marmalade, black coffee), and read two newspapers (in an easy chair, with his feet up on an ottoman) until 8:45 A.M. Between then and 10 A.M. he did some light desk work and made a few telephone calls. At 10 o'clock he shut off his phone, opened his mind and began to think."

Cowan begins thinking about a radio program from the past — *Take It or Leave It*, on the air from 1940-52.

The game on *Take It or Leave It* was *Who Wants to Be a Millionaire?* on a smaller level — a contestant won steadily increasing amounts of money for answering steadily more difficult questions. The prize for answering the first question is $1, and the contestant has the option of taking on another question for double the money, up to $64, or he/she can stop and take the money earned to that point.

For most of its run, *Take It or Leave It* is a Sunday-night staple, as much a part of America's listening habits on that night as comics Jack Benny, Edgar Bergen and Charlie McCarthy and Fred Allen. The host is vaudeville comic-musician Phil Baker, who isn't above giving clues to help contestants guess the correct answer — especially if the contestants are active-duty servicemen.

The top money question on *Take It or Leave It* is the $64 question, and the phrase becomes a part of the American vernacular — so much so that in 1950 it becomes the show's title.

"The $64 wasn't enough to make news" on the new show, Cowan tells *The New York Times*. "$640? That's nothing, either. Nor is $6,400. But $64,000 gets into the realm of the almost impossible. Once I had that, I knew just what was going to happen."[22]

But beyond the money and the format, Cowan adds an additional element borrowed from his best-known creation, *Quiz Kids*. A question-answer show similar to *Information Please*, it features regular panelists all under the age of 16 and extraordinarily gifted in areas such as music, mathematics, or a branch of science. Each week they easily answer the complicated/esoteric questions sent in by listeners and become celebrities of a sort. Listeners tune in each week because of the personalities as much as the quiz.

The $64,000 Question will be personality-focused as well. It will be designed so that each successful contestant can be on the air as long as five weeks in the quest for cash, prolonging the suspense and giving the audience the chance to take him/her to their hearts.

"My absolutely firm feeling about reality on TV," Cowan tells *The New York Times*, "is that there's too little of it. . . . I wanted to set up an event where people would be tremendously interested, would care what happened, and not know until it happened what was going to happen."[23]

Writes David Halberstam: "The concept depended on the belief that seemingly unexceptional Americans did indeed have secret talents and secret knowledge. That appealed greatly to Cowan, who, with his Eastern European Jewish background, had a highly idealized view of his fellow citizens' potential to reach beyond the apparent limits life had dealt them. His was an idealistic, almost innocent belief in the ordinary people of the country. . . . With his generous and optimistic nature, he saw the show as emblematic of the American dream; it offered everyone not only a chance to become rich every night, but to win the esteem of his fellow citizens."[24]

Cowan's wife, Polly, is not as convinced the show will be a success, and she isn't the only one.

When Cowan tells game-show producer Mark Goodson his idea, Goodson tells him, "The only way this show is going to work is if it's rigged."[25]

But Cowan perseveres.

Says Joseph Cates, producer of *The $64,000 Question*: "Lou Cowan is the only man who ever said to me, in forty-odd years, when he employed me, he said, 'The most important thing to me is my good name. I'll back you in everything, in anything that comes up, as long as you don't dishonor my good name.' "26

Cowan's representative, Steve Carlin, begins pitching *The $64,000 Question* to the ad agencies representing the sponsors who still control much of the programming on radio and TV.

But his first efforts meet with disappointment.

Cosmetics magnate Helena Rubinstein turns down the idea, reportedly because she doesn't have a TV and doesn't recognize the sales power of the medium. Chrysler executives also decline, fearing that funding a game show with big cash prizes will cause resentment among their unionized workforce when it comes to bargaining for raises. The Lewyt Vacuum Cleaner Company turns it down because it's felt that TV is better at selling impulse items, not $79 household appliances.27

Finally Carlin meets with Walter Craig.

Craig: The Pitchman

An ex-vaudevillian and a vice president at what was known at that point as the William Weintraub advertising agency, Walter Craig is described by *Sponsor* magazine as a "dapper Madison Avenueite who lives and breathes show business. Says he about his only child, a seven-and-a-half year old girl: 'She uses the right words in the right places, and she's learned her vocabulary from TV.' "28

Craig is looking for a show for a notoriously hard-to-please client — Revlon. And as Carlin pitches, Craig immediately sees the possibilities.

"Lou Cowan brought us the idea," Craig will say later, "and I locked myself and some of the boys into a conference room from 9:00 a.m. until 3:00 a.m., with the idea on paper. I said, 'No one leaves till it's signed,' and so we worked the bugs out of it."29

In an unusual move, Craig uses the agency's money, rather than the client's money, to buy the idea. He and partner Norman Nor-

man (not a typo) are that convinced it can be something special —
for another client if Revlon declines. The show's concept perfectly
fits the agency's sales strategy, as developed by Norman — to sell
through empathy, specifically through a philosophy with the acronym PEOPLE:

- Put people in the sell
- Excitingly different look and sound
- Open the way through the heart, not the head
- Put in an important reason why
- Living visuals people will talk about
- Eliminate any non-preemptive selling proposition[30]

The $64,000 Question will have everything — human drama,
cliffhanger endings, suspense, money as a reward for knowledge,
and Cadillac convertibles given away as consolation prizes.

As for the show's dramatic content, it will begin from the
moment a contestant walks on stage "on the golden threshold," as
an announcer continually reminds us.

After a bit of small talk with Hal March, the contestant chooses a
particular category, and the first four questions — worth $64, $128,
$256, and $512 — are selected from those shuffled by a spank-
ing-new IBM computer. It looks dramatic, but all the cards con-
tain the same question. (And the question is written phonetically to
accommodate Hal March's learning disorder.)[31]

The next level — questions worth $1,000, $2,000 and $4,000
——- are taken from a prominently-marked Diebold (product place-
ment) safe, from which Ben Feit, a vice-president of the Manufac-
turers Trust Company (the bank where Revlon does its business),
hands them to emcee Hal March.

Feit is flanked by uniformed guards, which seems a little extreme
in retrospect. But the public eats it up. Feit himself is promoted
weeks after the show premieres.[32]

Once they have correctly answered questions that reach the $8,000 level, contestants enter the isolation booth.

The ones who answer the question at the $16,000 plateau have until next week's show to decide about either going forward to $32,000 or leaving with their winnings. Same with winning $32,000 — contestants have another week to decide, and Revlon has another week to keep America watching and buying.

Consciously or not, *The $64,000 Question* is almost a perfect illustration of Norman Norman's PEOPLE sales strategy. By presenting "living visuals" through humble yet educated contestants with their own vivid interests and unique uses for the prize money, the show makes viewers feel good about themselves and about America in general.

Once he buys *The $64,000 Question*, Craig faces the next step — selling the idea to the mercurial Revson.

Revson: The Sponsor

Charles Haskell Revson is always immaculately groomed, in dark suits and ties, and expects his underlings to follow his example. He once dropped an advertising agency because the executive servicing his account had dirty fingernails. (The ad man had replied, "What do you want me to do? Wear nail polish?" Revson laughed and then fired him.)[33]

One day another account executive has the misfortune to wear a brown plaid suit to the office. Revson shoots him a look and says, "Kiddie, you know what brown's the color of? Get out."[34]

Says Steve Carlin, executive producer of *The $64,000 Question*: "Charlie Revson was the kind of man who walked into a room and gave the impression that everyone was farting, and he was the only total gentleman."[35]

Revson is known for his imperious yet morose manner and a bulldog mug that looks like a cross between actor Edward G. Robinson and one-time Alabama governor George Wallace. He is the public face of Revlon — the entrepreneur, the decision maker, the closer, the enforcer.

He formed Revlon in 1932 with two other partners, one of which was his brother, Martin. They had grown up in a working-class neighborhood in Manchester, New Hampshire, where their father made a meager living as a cigar roller. With just a high school education, Revson goes from selling nail polish to beauty salons to building a giant corporation. And between 1944 and 1957, Revlon burns through nine separate advertising agencies.

"In the annals of American business," writes Andrew Tobias in his Revson biography, *Fire and Ice*, "Revson has to be compared not with Helena Rubinstein and Elizabeth Arden, though those comparisons are themselves fascinating, but with staggering egomaniacs like Walt Disney or even the original Henry Ford. *Big*-time sons of bitches."[36]

Under Revson's leadership, Revlon prospers with the help of extensive color advertising in magazines. By 1953 it's outpacing all of its competitors, including Max Factor, Helena Rubenstein and Coty.

Still, Revson is suffering from television envy — more specifically, an envy of competitor Hazel Bishop, the sponsor of TV's self-described "most talked-about program," NBC's *This Is Your Life*, which exists in the rarefied company of *I Love Lucy* and *Dragnet* at the top of the TV ratings.

To Revson, ratings aren't all that important, but sales are. And in 1953, Hazel Bishop sales reach $10 million, largely due to its sponsorship of *This Is Your Life*.

Each week, *This Is Your Life* host Ralph Edwards surprises a celebrity — someone in show business or involved in world events — by telling his or her life story, highlighted by emotional reunions with family and friends, as the celebrity sits on the "Hazel Bishop stage," dotted with the Hazel Bishop logo, in between commercials for Hazel Bishop No-Smear Lipstick.[37]

The millions watching *This Is Your Life* see a prominent Hazel Bishop presence on camera *all through the show*. By contrast, Revlon is co-sponsoring the anthology series *Danger* on CBS, and Revlon's presence is confined just to commercials — every other week at that. So when Walter Craig pitches, Charles Revson listens — Hazel Bishop's example has taught him the advantage of showcasing your brand in front of the viewing public for an entire show, even if it's in simple black and white.

***

On March 16, 1955, the announcement comes in *The New York Times*:

$64,000 QUIZ BOWS
IN JUNE ON C.B.S.
Revlon Will Sponsor Largest
TV Cash Jackpot – Show
Planned for Tuesdays

Despite the possibility of a large payout of prize money, *The $64,000 Question* will still only cost half as much to produce per episode as *This Is Your Life*. And as the sole sponsor, Revlon is featured prominently — in everything from elaborate TV commercials staged like Hollywood musicals to the huge REVLON name and lipsticks on the show's isolation booth to the prominence of the company name on the show's logo (it is, on your screen, "Revlon's $64,000 Question").

Revson's decision to go with the show does not come without misgivings. "He was getting awfully tired of investing in one 'stiff' of a TV series after the next," wrote Tobias. "He had a natural bias against television advertising, anyway. It was in black and white, and he was selling colors. Nor could he control TV ads the way he could control print."[38]

Within weeks after its debut, *The $64,000 Question* will become the highest-rated show on the largest advertising medium in the world — the CBS television network.[39]

But that is not yet apparent when the show premieres. And Revson, characteristically looking on the dark side, insists on the right to pull out after 13 weeks if the show is a dud.

CHAPTER TWO: "THE PROGRAM WHERE KNOWLEDGE IS KING AND THE REWARD KING-SIZED" (JUNE-DECEMBER 1955)

"Revlon, the greatest name in cosmetics, presents the show
where knowledge is king and the reward king-sized:
The one — two —- four — yes,
the sixty-four thousand dollar question!"
— Announcer's opening from
The $64,000 Question, summer 1955

Why do we watch what we watch on TV?

A thousand different people will give you two thousand different answers. And today, thanks to technological advances, they might watch TV on a dozen or more different devices, on any number of streaming services.

By contrast, in television's early days, you watch a show on one screen — a TV set. Most households have only one, if that, and it's usually in a central location, such as a living room, where viewers gather the way cavemen gathered around a campfire. The experience is communal, especially when it comes to a TV event deemed culturally or historically important. There's even a phrase for it — "watercooler TV," an artifact from an age when there were fewer TVs and fewer TV channels to choose from, and when offices had water coolers around which employees would congregate and talk about the show they all watched last night. (Similarly, in the late 1990s NBC dubbed its Thursday night lineup of hit sitcoms "Must-See TV.")

Today there are so many different shows, channels, video games, social media outlets and streaming services — and so many different kinds of screens on which to watch them — that the big, inescapable must-watch show that draws a huge, diverse audience may only happen once a year, if that often — a Super Bowl, for instance, or the finale of a long-running series.

In the 1950s, by contrast, the choices are more limited and, perhaps because of that, the programs seem more important. The first example of water-cooler TV is the medium's first major hit, said to be responsible for the sale of thousands of sets — *Texaco Star Theatre*, a weekly variety show that runs on NBC from 1948-53. It makes a worldwide star of its host, comic Milton Berle, dubbed "Mr. Television." (The show is also said to be responsible for spikes in water usage not related to a cooler – America collectively refrains from using the restroom until Mr. Television is off the air, and then they rush en masse for the john.)

In 1951, *I Love Lucy* premieres and instantly becomes water-cooler TV, particularly the episode where Lucy Ricardo (Lucille Ball) gives birth to a son on TV (and in real life the next day). "Lucy Goes to the Hospital," which airs on January 19, 1953, receives a 71.7 Nielsen rating. Today, by contrast, to demonstrate how fragmented the TV audience is, the most popular prime-time show usually has an 18 rating or less.

At least at first, *The $64,000 Question* isn't water-cooler TV. The show premieres just as TV's summer doldrums are about to begin, and the only drawing card is the cash. In *Billboard*, Jack Singer says, "[q]uiz shows have always relied successfully on their giveaway aspects to attract audiences. And this being the biggest giveaway of them all, there's no reason why viewers shouldn't flock to it in droves." Singer also wishes that Hal March would jazz things up more, a la the hyperkinetic, patronizing manner of Bert Parks, who at that point, before his days as the host of the Miss America pageant, is best known as the energetic host of the game shows *Break the Bank* and *Stop the Music*.[1]

"Even in these inflationary times," writes the critic for *Variety*, "$64,000 in cash adds up to spectacular loot for answering questions correctly. With this kind of exciting coin involved, there'll be an audience around. . . . Hal March registered as a highly personable emcee who knows how to interject an ad lib without interfering with the pace of the stanza. . . . The plugs for the cosmetic product were handled effectively by a series of live model shots and straight pitches. Plenty of sell."[2]

The first contestant on the first broadcast is Thelma Bennett, a New Jersey housewife who works her way up to the $4,000 level in the category of movies. She then misses a question and makes her exit behind the wheel of a Cadillac convertible — pushed away by stagehands. (Note to self: Frank Capra was the director of *It Happened One Night*, in case a quiz show asks.)[3]

The second contestant on the first show will be the first one to hit the headlines — Redmond O'Hanlon, 39, a patrolman with the New York City Police Department and an expert on Shakespeare. His (literal) blue-collar job belies his erudite background — he has a Master's degree from Fordham University.

O'Hanlon wins $8,000 on that episode and is scheduled to return in a week. Three days later, he's the subject of a feature item in *The New York Times*, which names *The $64,000 Question* in a way that would warm Charles Revson's cold heart:

"On the Revlon show, for which he applied last March," the article says, "O'Hanlon took the eight questions in easy, scholarly stride. His Shakespearean delivery is delightfully flavored with West Side, but you feel his complete assurance.

"[I]t's fascinating," O'Hanlon tells the reporter, "when you stop to think that $64,000 is probably much more than Will made with all his plays and all his acting, in all his years."[4]

Just after the first episode goes off the air, Charles Revson makes his displeasure known.

Producer Joseph Cates tells an interviewer in the early 1990s: "I distinctly remember . . . Charles Revson, who owned Revlon, stood in the booth behind me — I heard him say to Walter Craig, of Norman, Craig & Kummel, the advertising agency, ' . . . that's another stiff you bought on my account. This thing is terrible,' and he walked out of there mumbling and grumbling."[5]

Revson then goes to one of his regular haunts, Billy Reid's Little Club, with brother Martin and Craig's partner Norman Norman, where they talk into the night, convincing Charles Revson to stay with the show.[6]

Someone else is also paying attention — legendary CBS news reporter/commentator Edward R. Murrow. The timeslot of the news show Murrow hosts, *See It Now*, is in close proximity to *The $64,000 Question*.

Said *See It Now* producer Fred W. Friendly, "We were in the control room when they ran the first *$64,000 Question*. Ed said to me, 'Any bets on how long we keep this time period now?' He was right, and we were soon off altogether. [CBS] knew they could sell the time for more money than they were getting from [*See It Now* sponsor] Alcoa."[7]

On the next Tuesday, June 14, O'Hanlon returns and, by answering correctly about the date of the printing of Shakespeare's first folio, wins $16,000. Audiences are beginning to pay attention — the show makes it into the Top 10 for the first time.

Then America waits for another week until June 21, when O'Hanlon announces his decision about whether he will try for $32,000 or leave with the $16,000.

Demonstrating a touch of the poet himself, O'Hanlon says, "The conservatism of a father of five has overruled the egotism of the scholar." He leaves with the sixteen grand.

The first big winner on *The $64,000 Question* is Redmond O'Hanlon,
pictured here with wife Marguerite. A New York beat cop who is also an
expert on Shakespeare, he wins $16,000 and declines to go any further —
"The conservatism of a father of five," he says, "has overruled the egotism of
the scholar."

By this point, three weeks into its run, *The $64,000 Question* is
far and away TV's number-one show, racking up a share of the audience almost double that of its nearest competitors.

"[T]he program has been clobbering the opposition," *Billboard*
reports in August, "and is currently number one in the rating
parade. It has received reams of publicity and is the most talked-
about new property in TV since *Disneyland*. . . . [S]ponsors and
agencies are beginning to re-evaluate their attitude toward quiz and
novelty shows."[8]

Cowan's format seems foolproof — a contestant's saga can stretch
over multiple weeks, and on every show there is a combination of a
"veteran" contestant trying for ever-more money and a newcomer
reaching for the heights.

"It's not merely the big money, it's the people," adman Walter
Craig says in a 1955 interview. "When they see the cop with his five
kids trying for something they get interested in his fortune."[9]

The show's next folk hero — or heroine —– appears for the first
time on July 11. Her name is Catherine E. Kreitzer, a grandmother

and clerical worker from Pennsylvania. She's written to the show's producers: "If you add the Bible as a category, you will have your first $64,000 winner."[10]

Kreitzer's run stretches over four weeks and everyone, it seems, is following her progress. Newspapers dub her "The Good Book Gal."[11] Reports *TV Guide*: "George Burns, Gracie Allen, Jack Benny and Mary Livingstone were vacationing in New York recently. They had arranged one evening to see *Bus Stop*, a hit Broadway show. Suddenly Benny remembered that on that same night Mrs. Catherine E. Kreitzer was to appear for her final round on *The $64,000 Question*. They immediately cancelled their *Bus Stop* reservations and stayed at their hotel to see whether Mrs. Kreitzer would take her $32,000 or go on to the $64,000 question."[12]

Bible expert Catherine Kreitzer is dubbed "The Good Book Gal" during her run to ultimately win $32,000 on *The $64,000 Question*.

Kreitzer stops at $32,000 on the August 2 show — but not before she, too, has become a national celebrity. Her son Ira, stationed at Loring Air Force Base in northeastern Maine, is treated like a VIP and transported to WTWO in Bangor so that he can watch his mother on TV.[13]

Again, the story makes nationwide headlines and delights the public. A Revlon executive reports that he was in a bar on the night of one of Kreitzer's appearances and the customers demanded that the TV be switched from a ballgame to the quiz show, whistling and cheering for Kreitzer.[14]

Kreitzer then visits *The Ed Sullivan Show* to chat with the host and read a chapter from Philippians starting with "Let your moderation be known unto all men," on which she says she based her decision not to try for the $64,000.[15] There is talk of her hosting a show, *The Bible and Mrs. Kreitzer*.[16]

At about the same time yet another media darling takes the stage — Gino Prato, a cobbler from 158th street in the Bronx, who has chosen opera as his category based on his lifelong love of the subject. He tells the TV audience of his interest in playing the accordion, his collection of 300 opera records, and of standing in line for two hours to get standing-room seats at the Metropolitan Opera. He throws kisses to the applauding multitudes when he answers questions correctly.

On July 25, Prato appears to announce whether he will try for $16,000. His voice, he explains to America, is hoarse because he's been preparing by singing arias all week. He tells the audience he is continuing to compete so that he can take his wife Caroline and daughter Lorraine to see his father in Italy, who they've never met.

Gino Prato, a cobbler from the Bronx, is another contestant on *The $64,000 Question* to become a household name. An expert in opera, his story unfolds over several weeks until he decides to stop with winnings of $16,000 after an emotional long-distance talk with his father in Italy — one that he recounts onstage to an enthralled America.

By now, Prato is a national celebrity. Reports one fan magazine:

"It wasn't just his opera information which intrigued people, it was his devotion to music, his modesty, his honesty, his charm. The president of a certain respected research firm, cruising the Hudson on his yacht, requested total silence from his guests while Gino was on the air. A television critic told of a professional intellectual — who, he suspected, owned a television set only so that he might condemn the programs — who now confessed shame-facedly that he had become a fan. A tough-mug taxi driver spoke for less double-domed viewers. 'You know about that guy Prato? The one with the operas? I tell you, my wife's gone buggy about that guy. You know, she even went to church and lit a candle for Prato?' "[17]

On August 2, Prato wins $32,000 by answering the following question:

"Giuseppe Verdi wrote an opera which later, incidentally, launched Arturo Toscanini as a conductor because of the illness of the regular conductor. Name the opera, the country where young Toscanini conducted it, the city in which it had its world premiere and give the eve of what holiday it occurred."

Prato rattles off the facts: "*Aida*; Brazil; Cairo, Egypt; Christmas Eve ... December 24, 1871."[18]

After Prato wins $32,000, all America waits a week to see whether he will try for $64,000. On August 9, Prato returns to the show and reads a letter from his father in Italy. He reads it in Italian, then he translates: His father says, "Stop where you are."

"Because all my life I take my Daddy's advice," Prato tells Hal March and virtually all of America, "I take it — the money. . . . Maybe I know the answers to some more questions. But maybe, if I lose, I give my papa a shock and it will kill him. I want to see my papa when I go to Italy. My papa, he call me a hard-head — stubborn. So I be a soft-head now."

"God bless you, Gino!" exclaims March.[19]

After his win on *The $64,000 Question*, Gino Prato travels to his native Italy to be welcomed as a hero (left), see his father (right), and have an audience with the Pope. Then he returns to America and is a guest on *The Perry Como Show*.

Prato's climactic appearance results in the show's best ratings yet — 72 percent of TV sets in use, or about 30 million viewers.[20]

The news even makes *The New York Times* — which, by now, covers the show as a regular weekly event. Prato then visits Italy and is hailed as a hero. He sees his father for the first time in 32 years. He's granted an audience with the Pope. Back in America, he appears on Perry Como's TV show. He's credited for a rise in interest in opera — the airline Swissair, which offers a European opera tour, reports that inquiries for the tour have more than doubled after Prato's appearance.[21]

A cobbler by trade, Prato is signed to become a goodwill ambassador for the American Biltrite Rubber Co, which makes shoemakers' supplies. He appears as a VIP to open the Pittsburgh Opera season and receives season passes to the Metropolitan Opera.[22]

***

"For roughly $35,000 a week, which takes in all charges except time," writes Jack Hellman in *Daily Variety*, "Revlon is getting the hottest bargain in tv [sic] with *The $64,000 Question*, the cost-per-thousand homes tabbed at $4."[23]

The cost is low, and Revlon's return is high. An article in *Television* magazine gives the details:

Frosted Nail Enamel is up 300%.

Living Lipstick is going 100% better than expected since it was launched on the opening broadcast. Revlon fell so far behind on orders for this item, it yanked the TV commercial by September. In October it was still about a month behind.

Satin Set is doing about 75% better than expected.

Lanolite Lipstick was featured only during the first month, yet maintains an increase of nearly 40%.

Revlon's Eye Makeup is only mentioned in the opening billboard of the program, yet its sales have jumped 45%. Similarly, Aquamarine Lotion, normally a cold-weather item, increased 10-15% through the summer.

In lipsticks, Revlon, long the leader, is leaving the competition far behind. In the spring, a national survey showed it running neck and neck with Hazel Bishop for first place in share of market. Revlon's share was about 25%, Bishop's about 21%.

By the end of July, Revlon's market share is said to have passed 30% while Bishop's had fallen to 14%. The next surveys are expect to show Revlon moving toward 40%.[24]

Revlon sales rise 54 percent in 1955, and another 66 percent in 1956. "We could have sold urine in a bag," admits Revlon advertising man Jay Bennett.[25] Meanwhile, the sales of Revlon competitor Hazel Bishop — the company whose sponsorship of the successful *This Is Your Life* TV series prompted Revson to get into television — sink like a stone.

Revlon products are sold in commercials moderated by such spokeswomen as Barbara Britton or Wendy Barrie.

"I like the show," Barbara Britton tells *TV Guide*, "because on it I get to look so pretty."[26]

The spots are done on live television, and hardly ever limited to just one minute.

"We would run 'sixty-second' commercials for *three minutes* and there was nothing they could do about it," a Revlon executive told Revson biographer Tobias. "What were they going to do? Run to the middle of the stage and yell, 'Stop!'? So there were times when we were literally running three-minute one-minute commercials. I think we ran over three minutes once."[27]

Barbara Britton was one of the spokeswoman for the elaborate, often overtime Revlon commercials on *The $64,000 Question*.

Sponsor magazine reports that a "boiling session" is held between attorneys for CBS and Revlon in order to get the cosmetic firm's commercials on *The $64,000 Question* down to the time required by the network. Revlon's commercials are running four and even five minutes long, prompting complaints from agencies with competitive accounts.[28]

Live TV also leads to commercial flubs: In one spot, live ducklings swim the wrong way, off-camera, and are grabbed by a quick-thinking model. In another, a model is supposed to utter the line, "Soap on my face? Never!" and it comes out "Face on my soap? Never!"

Then there are darker moments that happen live — during one broadcast, someone walks in off the street and knifes a cameraman. Another time, an Hungarian freedom fighter somehow makes it onto the stage, and a quick-thinking Hal March ushers him off camera.[29]

Just as Gino Prato departs, Gloria Lockerman begins a short but successful run on the show.

A 12-year-old African-American student from Baltimore who lives with her grandparents, Lockerman's specialty is spelling, and on August 16 she wins the $8,000 prize for spelling "antidisestablishmentarianism," turning that term into a temporary household word. The next week, for $16,000, she spells correctly the entire sentence "The belligerent astigmatic anthropologist annihilated innumerable chrysanthemums."

Once she reaches the $16,000 level, Gloria decides to take her winnings and step aside. "I'd rather be Gloria the undefeated champion than Gloria the girl who lost," she says on August 30.[30] She later will appear as a guest on Martha Raye's NBC variety show, along with Tallulah Bankhead. Certain viewers complain to the network when Bankhead affectionately holds Lockerman's hand on the air.[31] She'll also be named one of *Mademoiselle* magazine's "Ten Young Women of the Year" and speak at the 1956 Democratic National Convention.[32]

In the fall of 1955, a few months after the debut of *The $64,000 Question*, popular television shows return to the air after a summer hiatus. But despite the reappearance of number-one show *I Love Lucy*, *The $64,000 Question* elbows Lucy aside and remains atop the ratings. And the decision is made to air the show live nationwide — because on the west coast, where viewers see a delayed broadcast, newscasts are scooping the show by reporting on the winners before the program airs.[33]

Meanwhile, waiting in the wings is the first contestant to go for the top prize: U.S. Marine Corps Captain Richard McCutcheon, a tall, beaming, lantern-jawed leatherneck whose specialty is cooking.

McCutcheon's stay on *The $64,000 Question* results in the program's highest ratings ever, and on September 13, 1955 he is asked by March whether he'll go for $64,000.

"I've known my decision for a long time," McCutcheon says. "I belong to a very proud organization, and the answer is 'Go.' "[34]

Almost 59 million people are watching at home as McCutcheon steps into the isolation booth.[35] March marches over to get the question from bank official Ben Feit.

The scene is played for maximum drama. With a tremble in his voice, March reads:

"Identify five dishes and two wines on the now famous menu of a royal banquet given in 1939 by King George VI for French President Albert Lebrun."

McCutcheon answers shakily, but steadily:

"Consomme is a broth of either meat, fish or fowl stock, Quenelle is what is called a force meat, a meat, fish or fowl dumpling. Truite saumonee is trout born —hatched — in fresh water, which migrated to the sea and returned. Steelhead, we call them in this country. Filet is a boneless cut. Maltaise is a hollandaise sauce with orange juice and a little orange peel in it. Petits Pois Francais are little garden peas with onion chopped up, with sugar and with butter. Corbelle is a pure French word meaning either a basket of fruit or a basket of flowers, so let's say a basket of fruit. Chateau y'quiem is a sweet dessert wine from the Bordeaux region of Sauterne. Madeira Sercial is a dry wine from the Maderia Islands. I believe the grapes are sercial and that is how it gets its name."[36]

"You ARE ABSOLUTELY RIGHT!" March shouts. The audience shouts and applauds wildly. Charles Revson steps on camera with a check for $64,000. At a convention of wholesale druggists in White Sulphur Springs, West Virginia, an attendee yells out, "The Marine has answered the question!"[37]

"If you're symbolic of the Marine Corps, Dick," says Hal March, "I don't see how we'll ever lose any battles."[38]

By flawlessly describing the menu for an elaborate royal dinner,
U.S. Marine Captain Richard McCutcheon — a cooking expert
— becomes the first top winner on *The $64,000 Question*.
Here he and emcee Hal March express their mutual admiration.

The story is on the front page of *The New York Times* the next morning and tax experts are interviewed, telling us that $31,150 of the money will go to Uncle Sam.[39] Meanwhile, the Hotel New Yorker adds the royal menu to its restaurant offerings. The tab is $2.95.[40]

McCutcheon's victory leads columnists and celebrities alike to rhapsodize over the contestants.

"It's not the money — it's those people!," actress Loretta Young tells *TV Guide.* "Gino Prato and that little Gloria and that wonderful Marine captain. All you read about in the papers is robbery and murder and juvenile delinquency and sex, and you begin to get the feeling that the whole human race is just no good. And then this show comes along and lets us see real, genuine people — a shoemaker and a little girl and a Marine, with all their wonderful qualities of sincerity and warmth and good humor — and it revives your faith in human nature."[41]

Adds columnist Joe Csida in *Sponsor* magazine: "I was watching the show with my wife, my daughter, who's 17 and just entering college, and my boy, who's nine. My family, I believe, is as normal in their reactions to TV entertainment as any . . . to a person, we literally thrilled to the Captain's crack at, and capture of, the loot."[42]

The influence of *The $64,000 Question* is all over the TV schedule. Five days after McCutcheon's win, the season premiere of the *Colgate Variety Hour*, hosted by Dean Martin and Jerry Lewis, features a *$64,000 Question* parody with Lewis as a hapless contestant dunked into a water tank instead of an isolation booth and Martin as emcee "Hal April." Revlon and its ad agency sue the team, alleging plagiarism and dilution of sponsor identification.[43]

On the CBS anthology series *Studio One*, Jackie Gleason appears in a drama called "Uncle Ed and Circumstance," about a downtrodden soul who wins $64,000 on the show, the set of which is reproduced in exact detail. (John Baragrey replaces Hal March as the emcee.)[44]

Existing programs add contests and jackpots to lure audiences. Dodge, the sponsor of *The Lawrence Welk Show*, introduces a contest in which the person who writes the best safety slogan will win a new car every year. *Truth or Consequences* and *Stop the Music* up their prize money and another CBS quiz, *The Big Payoff*, offers a mink coat, a trip to Europe, a convertible and a diamond ring to the person who correctly guesses the number of sequins on a model's bathing suit. Groucho Marx announces that when someone says the secret word on *You Bet Your Life*, he or she will win $101 instead of $100.[45]

And on October 8 comes NBC's entry in the big-money quiz sweepstakes. It's called *The Big Surprise* and it's produced by Lou Cowan's company. (Cowan himself isn't involved — due to the success of *The $64,000 Question* he's become VP of Creative Services for CBS.) The new show attempts to showcase common-man contestants in the manner of *The $64,000 Question*, and adds a larger grand prize of $100,000. But *The Big Surprise* doesn't catch on. Critics say the format, which includes a teletype machine and complicated riddles, is too cluttered. Some say they don't care for the show's host, Jack Barry. He is replaced by future *60 Minutes* co-host Mike Wallace, but the show still struggles.

Says *Sponsor* magazine: "Missing . . . from *The Big Surprise* is the natural story quality of paradox; in other words, the switch: the shoemaker who knows opera, the cop who knows Shakespeare. *Big Surprise* contestants start out answering questions about their own past, a subject they should know. . . . If the show overcomes those obstacles, it will encourage other imitators; there's no patent on giving nice people money."[46]

"If this is NBC's answer to *$64,000 Question*," opines *Daily Variety*, "it won't get past the first plateau. . . . Its only excuse seems to be, 'Give away more than $64,000 and get a bigger rating.' Not a chance."[47]

Meanwhile, *The $64,000 Question* rolls on; Myrtle Power is the next contestant to capture the public's imagination. A 70-year-old grandmother from Buford, Georgia, her category is baseball, and she's on the show just as the playoffs are beginning. Over a period of several weeks, with her family in the audience, Myrt, as she asks Hal March to call her, wins $32,000. For that September 20 broadcast, television sets are installed in baseball stadiums around the country.

At the end of the show, March reminds Myrt that she has a week to decide whether or not she'll go for the $64,000. "Want me to answer it now?," asks the media-savvy Myrt.

Myrtle "Myrt" Power, a 70-year-old grandmother, wins $32,000 by answering questions about baseball on *The $64,000 Question*. In the foreground is a bust of Myrt created by an admiring art professor.

"No, not now," says March with a laugh. "You almost blew a whole program, Myrt."[48]

Next week, Myrt says she'll take the $32,000 and run.

***

As contestant after contestant crosses "the golden threshold" on *Question*, something darker is happening behind the scenes — there is a serious, and shady, effort afoot to move *The $64,000 Question* from CBS to NBC.[49]

The offer is massive — in exchange for the move, Revlon would receive the equivalent of $2 million a year in free daytime advertising on NBC, extra promotion of all Revlon-sponsored shows and a timeslot for a *$64,000 Question* spinoff.

In other words, it's a massive giveaway to lure television's biggest giveaway show.

The offer raises eyebrows on Madison Avenue. Reports *Variety*: "One top consultant, whose clients' billings run into multi-millions, said . . . that he would advise them to demand 'equal free time' from

NBC under the same terms the network is reportedly offering it to Revlon. He said NBC is setting a 'dangerous' precedent in giving away time to secure a program."[50]

In the heat of the moment it's not totally clear from where the NBC overture originated.

The first story is that it was made to placate a powerful NBC client — the advertising agency Batten, Barton, Durstine & Osborn, or BBD&O, on behalf of *their* client. Armstrong Cork. The story goes that the offer is made because by moving *The $64,000 Question* from its Tuesday night slot on CBS, it would no longer compete with *Armstrong Circle Theatre* on NBC.[51]

A few days later, however, it becomes clear that the entire affair was orchestrated not by BBD&O, or NBC, or even Armstrong Cork, but by Revlon.[52]

"Revlon ultimately decided to stay with CBS," Revson biographer Tobias writes, "but not before *Variety* had summed up the battle as 'the most extravagant power play in TV's annals.' Agencies and sponsors, *Variety* wrote, 'are even yet salving wounded feeling as they recapitulate the most fantastic crisscross pattern and chain reaction of events that transcends anything that vets in the business can recall.' "[53]

And the fireworks aren't going to end anytime soon — at least not as far as Charles Revson is concerned.

In early December, right around the time that Norman, Craig & Kummel staffers are orchestrating a massive Revlon sales meeting at the Waldorf-Astoria to celebrate the company's banner year, the news comes that NC&K is inheriting a new account — Speidel watch bands.

So far, so good.

That means that NC&K will also inherit the production duties of the quiz show Speidel sponsors — *The Big Surprise.*

So far, so bad — at least as far as Charles and Martin Revson are concerned.

The brothers Revson give NC&K an ultimatum — forget Spiedel and focus solely on Revlon business through *The $64,000 Question* or lose the account for producing an additional quiz show — even though the show doesn't compete in any way with *The $64,000 Question*.[54]

All of this despite the fact that Revlon has been connected with NC&K for seven years, dating to when it was still known as the William Weintraub agency. And despite the fact that Revlon's recent spectacular success is directly connected to the expertise of NC&K, particularly VP Walter Craig, who saw the potential in *Question*.

"There wasn't any of that 'mutual agreement' nonsense," agency head Norman B. Norman tells *Advertising Age*. "We were canned. We got 30 days notice after seven years on the account."[55]

"The Revsons," wryly notes a report in *Variety*, "are known on the street for their nervousness, angles and short supply of personal attachment."[56]

The story goes on to say that the Revsons resented all the media attention given to Walter Craig and Lou Cowan as the guiding forces behind *The $64,000 Question*, and adds, "the Revsons have been pressuring Lou Cowan Inc. for changes in format and publicity but the latter office has been tough, refusing to rewrite a hit. There have been repeated clashes between the package owner (Cowan) and Revlon when the latter acted unilaterally in matters relating to the program. It has been laid on the line very firmly: **'You don't own this show, we do. You lease it.'** " (Emphasis by *Variety*.)[57]

The Revsons put their money where their mouths are and move their business to BBD&O. *The $64,000 Question* will still be sponsored by Revlon, but with the change in agency and with Cowan no longer playing an active role, there's a greater opportunity for the Revson brothers' wishes — regarding the show as well as the contestants who succeed on it — to prevail.

CHAPTER THREE: "STIFF HIM" (DECEMBER 1955-MARCH 1957)

*"What might be the final word on giveaways comes from
TV comedy writer-director Nat (Phil Silvers Show) Hiken,
who whimsically suggests a show called A Million or Your Life.
'The contestant will stand in front of the TV camera
and face two gun barrels. One will be loaded with a dud
containing a check for $1,000,000 — the other will be a live 37mm
shell guaranteed to tear his head off.' "*
— Time *magazine, September 3, 1956*

As 1955 nears its end, *The $64,000 Question* remains atop the TV ratings, and the company that sponsors it, Revlon, is experiencing double-digit sales increases — 1955 sales are 54% higher than 1954. Charles Revson announces that it's the yearly greatest dollar-volume growth in Revlon history.[1] Revlon stock goes public in December at $12 a share and hits $30 within a few weeks — thanks largely to *Question*.[2]

The show is also the subject of a study commissioned by the Norman, Craig & Kummel ad agency. Behavioral specialist Dr. Ernest Dichter concludes that viewers love the show because they yearn to emerge from anonymity as the contestants have done. Viewers find the show sincere, spontaneous and suspenseful and the contestants "real and natural."[3]

So on the surface, not much has changed. But as 1956 begins, things are different behind the scenes.

Lou Cowan, the original producer-packager of the show, is no longer involved on a day-to-day basis — he is now a vice president at CBS. And the ad agency Norman, Craig & Kummel, which bought the show for its client, Revlon, is shoved out of the picture when Revlon president Charles Revson decides to move his business to another agency — Batten, Barton, Durstine & Osborn (BBD&O).

(Comedian Fred Allen, no fan of advertising agencies because of their control over program content, once famously joked that Batten, Barton, Durstine & Osborn sounded like a wardrobe trunk falling down a flight of stairs.)[4]

The move to BBD&O means that for all practical purposes, Charles Revson now unilaterally runs *The $64,000 Question*. And as a man obsessed with success, with selling his products, he is always trying to figure out how the outcome of the show can be made to seem spontaneous and suspenseful every week, while in reality be carefully planned. If the new ad agency pushes back against his desires to control the show, whether through ultra-long commercials or by deciding which contestants will fail or succeed, he'll, again, just take his business somewhere else. (And he eventually will, breaking up Revlon's family of brands and moving them to four different agencies in 1958.)

After each *Question* broadcast, Revson and/or his brother Martin meet with Revlon executives and advertising men, where they either criticize contestants for being "boring" and order their downfalls, or mandate that a popular contestant stay on the shows, no matter what — Charles Revson has a chart that correlates ratings and sales figures. They never tell their underlings in so many words to blatantly rig the show's outcome, but they don't have to — their desires are crystal clear.

Says producer Joe Cates: "[Charles Revson] was an obsessive-compulsive guy. That's why he was successful. We had regular meetings with him, and he wanted to discuss each contestant, the performance the previous week, the contestants for next week. . . . If we agreed with Charlie that maybe a contestant's personality didn't come across, maybe less attention was paid to him in the routining; or they would put him on earlier, not in the big spot, or we would ask him a harder question, or simplify someone else's question."[5]

Mark Goodson, who with Bill Todman produced such game shows as *What's My Line?* and *The Price Is Right*, recalled being in a meeting where someone had to take a call from Revson.

"Somebody . . . said he had a call from Charlie Revson, and he left the meeting," Goodson said. "And when he came back he said, 'Listen, that's Charlie. Charlie wants, he thinks the Lincoln expert is boring. He wants you to stiff him. I remember that line — 'He thinks the Lincoln expert is boring. He wants you to stiff him.' "[6]

Question producer Mert Koplin: "We'd sit in sponsor's meetings and they'd say, 'We like that [contestant]! That one needs to go to 64!' or 'We don't like that one — let's get rid of him.' "[7]

But at least one contestant gets around Revson's manipulation.

In later years, Dr. Joyce Brothers will be a familiar face on TV talk and quiz shows, but at this point the petite psychologist is a college instructor and new mother. With Koplin's encouragement and blessing, she cleverly chooses an unlikely, attention-getting subject of expertise — boxing.

Brothers isn't really a boxing expert. But she knows that the world of boxing facts and trivia is a relatively narrow one, and can be easily memorized. It doesn't hurt that Nat Fleischer, the editor of *Ring* magazine and author of several books on boxing, is a friend of her father's, and can coach her.

With the guidance of Fleischer, Brothers gets down to work, while Revson, behind the scenes, tries to unseat her.

Koplin: "I had to face the 'Get rid of her! Get rid of her!' bit. She didn't fit in with their concept of what cosmetics were all about."[8]

Brothers uses her photographic memory to absorb the comparatively limited statistics about professional boxing, and becomes the show's first woman to win the $64,000 prize on December 6, 1955.

Dr. Joyce Brothers used her skill at memorization to become an expert in the limited field of boxing statistics. It leads to her winning $64,000, despite the displeasure of Charles Revson, sponsor of *The $64,000 Question*. Here Brothers poses with middleweight champ Carl "Bobo" Olson and challenger Sugar Ray Robinson before a bout in December 1955.

If there was any doubt, the show still holds its power over viewers. Because this particular episode runs over by more than 30 seconds, the ending — Brothers' last-minute win — is cut off on the west coast. Viewers flood the switchboards of TV stations wanting to know the outcome.[9]

Brothers cashes in on her fame — she accepts $1,000 to appear at a Toronto night club on New Year's Eve[10] and gets to work on a book about how to improve your memory.[11]

In February comes another contestant who, like Gino Prato, specializes in opera — with the help of Prato as adviser, Michael della Rocca wins $64,000. A cobbler like Prato, he says he will use the money to support an opera company. "I fix shoes for the bread of my son and I stage operas for the bread of my soul," he tells *The New York Times*.[12]

Another contestant, Mabel Morris, a welfare recipient with high blood pressure, quits at $32,000 on the advice of her physician. Mail carrier Roscoe Wright, who writes poetry on the side, donates part of his $16,000 winnings to his church's organ fund.[13]

Emcee Hal March is also getting a share of the spotlight. Fan magazines report on his life story and breathlessly cover his courtship of and marriage to model Candy Toxton, which happens as soon as her divorce from Mel Torme is final.[14] Bride and groom are interviewed by Edward R. Murrow on *Person to Person*.

Meanwhile, on Italian TV, *$64,000* quiz copy *Lascia o Radoppia* (Double or Nothing) is so popular that Italian film exhibitors force a schedule switch from Saturday to Thursday nights because weekend movie business is suffering.[15]

In the spring of 1956, Charles Revson's wish for the *Question* spinoff comes true.

The $64,000 Challenge, airing on Sunday night, features past winners of the *Question*, reintroducing contestants with proven audience popularity — Gloria Lockerman, Capt. Richard McCutcheon, Myrt Power, Gino Prato, Dr. Joyce Brothers. *The $64,000 Challenge* gives them a chance to win even more money by pitting two contestants against each other in isolation booths shaped like giant chess pieces. (The booths are in honor of the show's co-sponsor, Kent cigarettes, which uses a chess piece as its trademark.)

The first *Challenge* is on April 8, 1956, and the first contestants are Shakespeare expert Redmond O'Hanlon and baseball expert Myrt Power, each facing a competitor. An odd fluff occurs — host Sonny Fox asks O'Hanlon the name of Desdemona's father in *Othello*. O'Hanlon answers incorrectly — he says Polonius — but Fox doesn't correct him. After the show it's pointed out that Brabantio was Desdemona's father, while Polonius was the father of Ophelia in *Hamlet*, and accusations of rehearsal are flung around.[16]

Fox experiences a few more on-air stumbles after that, and as a result he is replaced by Ralph Story as emcee. But *The $64,000 Challenge* is still an immediate success.

The $64,000 Challenge, a spinoff of *Question*, debuts in the spring
of 1956 and is almost as popular as its predecessor. Soon after
the debut, Ralph Story (pictured here) replaces Sonny Fox as the host.

Right around the same time, jockey Billy Pearson is in the midst
of a six-week run on *The $64,000 Question*. His subject: art. His
total take: $64,000.[17] Almost immediately, he moves to *The $64,000
Challenge*, challenged by fellow art lover Vincent Price.

Jockey Billy Pearson, an art expert, won $170,000 on *The $64,000
Question* and *The $64,000 Challenge*. "I went on *The $64,000 Challenge*,"
he once said, "to pay make enough money to pay taxes on the money I'd
won on *The $64,000 Question*."

In the spring, when *Variety* announces its annual showmanagement review, a special citation goes to *Question*, on the cusp of its first anniversary:

"Not since Lucille Ball and *I Love Lucy* were preparing to have her baby together has a television show registered so sharply on the public consciousness as has *The $64,000 Question* this past season. . . . The key to the program's success is not so much in the size of the prize . . . but in the showmanly formula that allowed 'ordinary people' to prove their abilities as experts in particular fields. It was a far cry from the typical quiz show that treats its contestants like intellectual vacuums or pitiful welfare cases."[18]

In June, *The $64,000 Question* marks its one-year anniversary with the quick reappearance of some former winners in between commercials. Comments *Variety*: "The Revlon commercials are something: in fact, they are pure poetry. Last week's show plugged a new color, 'snow peach,' a look of pure allure that rocked the Riviera, all recited with a breathy passion worthy of the great classics."[19]

By July, *Question* is the number-one show on TV and *Challenge* is third.[20] When Danish explorer-writer Peter Freuchen wins $64,000 on *Question*, it makes the national press yet again.[21] It isn't explained why he doesn't just stay in Denmark to win on *The $64,000 Kroner*, unless it's because 64,000 kroner comes to only about $9,000.[22]

As another fall TV season approaches, new quiz show ideas are being hatched. One comes from producers Dan Enright and Jack Barry, who have had hits with *Juvenile Jury* and *Life Begins at 80*. The new show is called *Twenty-One* and it will be emceed by Barry, recently bumped from *The Big Surprise*.

Jack Barry, the host of *Twenty-One*. He and his producing
partner, Dan Enright, also worked together on *Life Begins at 80*,
Juvenile Jury, and *Winky Dink and You*.

On *Twenty-One*, two players compete against each other in the now-requisite isolation booths. A category is announced by Barry and each player, in turn, chooses a question worth between one and eleven points, based on its difficulty. Neither player knows which question the other is choosing, and if a player thinks he or she has more points than the opposing player, the player can quit at any time as long as the total is less than 21. A sponsor is found — Geritol, an iron tonic (and Geritol Jr. for the kids) — and a Wednesday night timeslot on NBC is secured.

Another new quiz idea comes from Charles Revson, the mogul who came so reluctantly to television. By now he's sold on the tube's ability to sell Revlon products. And he starts to wonder: With Revlon having such an outsized television presence on Sunday nights with *Challenge* and on Tuesday nights with *Question*, why not sponsor a Monday night show as well?

So a half-hour timeslot is bought on NBC. It's dirt cheap because it's opposite the still-potent *I Love Lucy* on CBS. The idea: *The Most Beautiful Girl in the World*, a season-long beauty contest with its own set of exclusive gimmicks, razzle-dazzle and big money — a $250,000 grand prize. Hal March is tabbed as emcee.[23]

Meanwhile, rumors begin to circulate about the honesty of quiz shows, and in September, *Question* executive producer Steve Carlin addresses them in *TV Guide*.

"Q.: Is *The $64,000 Question* rigged in any way?

"A.: Absolutely not. I will stake my entire reputation as a showman on this answer: *The $64,000 Question, The $64,000 Challenge* and *The Big Surprise* are completely honest. Even if we wanted to 'rig' the show, we simply could not afford to. One slip and we would be through forever. . . . [T]he only thing we stage on our shows is showmanship. . . . When the average American looks at *The $64,000 Question*, he is pleasantly shocked to discover how much his fellow American knows. It makes him feel good. That's our formula."[24]

Both *The $64,000 Question* and *The $64,000 Challenge* are now being peppered with celebrity appearances. Comedian Jack Benny, whose trademark is his bad violin playing and his legendary stinginess, appears on *Question* to answer questions on the subject of the violin. He successfully answers the first $64 question, takes the money and quits.[25] Jackie Coogan, later Uncle Fester on TV's *The Addams Family*, appears as an expert on silent movies on *The $64,000 Challenge* due to his role, as a child actor, opposite Charlie Chaplin in *The Kid*.[26] Also on *The $64,000 Challenge*, art expert Vincent Price gets a new challenger — art expert Edward G. Robinson. The square-off of the two actors nets big ratings, and also boosts ticket sales for *Middle of the Night*, the Broadway play in which Robinson is starring.[27]

***

Twenty-One is scheduled to debut on September 12, while premiere dates for *The Most Beautiful Girl in the World* are pushed back three different times.[28]

Finally, after much thought, Revson abandons the *Beautiful* idea.

For one thing, he's busy calling the shots on *Question* and *Challenge*. For another, could his "wishes" regarding contestants be carried out on *The Most Beautiful Girl in the World*, with its planned panel of judges? Not likely. And Revson might be cool to the idea of a show he can't manipulate.

***

The first broadcast of *Twenty-One* is embarrassingly slow and awkward. Rounds keep ending in scoreless ties as the studio audience groans and emcee Barry wipes his brow. Geritol executives picture sales plummeting as viewers across the country flip to other stations.

So, because it's thought to ensure success, the rigging of *Twenty-One* begins. But where the controls on *The $64,000 Question* are subtle, shaping questions to fit what producers call the contestants' "knowledge matrix," the producers of *Twenty-One* deliberately rehearse contestants — instructing them to take dives, or to answer questions incorrectly — and purposely tie game scores to keep the suspense growing from week to week.

Producer Dan Enright: "We felt that it had such great quality and content to it that we would not have to rig it. In fact, the first show of *Twenty-One* was not rigged, and the first show of *Twenty-One* was a dismal failure. It was just plain dull. It lacked all drama, it lacked all suspense. And next morning, the sponsor called my partner, Jack Barry, and me, and told us in no uncertain terms that he never wanted to see a repeat of what happened the previous night. And from that moment on, we decided to rig *Twenty-One*."[29]

Even despite the rigging, however, the contestants who win on *Twenty-One* are largely failing to interest the public, unlike the winners on *The $64,000 Question*.

Then comes a gentleman named Herbert Stempel. After he takes a test to qualify for the show and scores on the genius level, he receives a visit from Dan Enright.

"He came to the apartment," Stempel recalls, "and then all of a sudden he leaned back in the sofa and said, 'How would you like to make $25,000?' . . . And he said to me something in essence which was like, 'Play ball and we'll make sure you make $25,000.' I said fine, what do I have to do? He says first of all, he says, you're gonna be on the program tomorrow night. The whole idea was to make me appear like an ex-GI working his way through college. [I was] asked to put on this old ill-fitting suit and [get a] marine-type haircut which made me appear as what you would call today a nerd, a square. I was never to call the master of ceremonies, Jack Barry, Jack. I was always to call him Mr. Barry and be very very humble and very sheepish."[30]

Stempel is a curiosity even among the eccentric world of quiz show contestants. He's stocky and cool in manner. He's an unemployed dilettante, a self-proclaimed genius with a photographic memory who often spends his days at the movies. He doesn't have the warmth of Gino Prato, or the sassiness of Myrt Power, or the straight-arrow style of Captain Richard McCutcheon, all beloved contestants on *The $64,000 Question*. You don't picture him sharing the stage with Ed Sullivan or Perry Como. When he and *Twenty-One* host Jack Barry get together, it's like a meeting of two morticians.

But during the fall of 1956, Stempel beats one contestant after another and gets a reputation for his intelligence, if not his personality. "The information that this fella has stuck away in his cranium is just unbelievable," Barry says admiringly on one show.[31]

Stempel: "I used to go down to Enright's office every Wednesday afternoon before the show. Dan Enright would pull out cards with the questions and answers that would be used that evening. I ran through them, he would instruct me when to pause, when to mop my brow, everything was very carefully choreographed. The hardest part of the show was not remembering the answers, or knowing the answers, but rather remembering 'Mop your brow twice, count to ten and breathe heavily' — this was the hardest part of the show was remembering the stage directions, which Enright had choreographed."[32]

Stempel is putty in the hands of the *Twenty-One* staff, willingly doing everything they ask. On one broadcast, Stempel is told the answer to a certain question. He knows it is wrong, but he answers as he is directed, and is told it's correct. When calls come in from across the nation saying the answer is actually wrong, an embarrassed Barry apologizes to Stempel on the air and asks him a replacement question. No one seems to notice the uncanny coincidence in that not only did Stempel give the wrong answer, but that Barry told him it was correct.

As Stempel's winnings grow, so does his ego.

"As the weeks went by people began to recognize me more and more, I got more and more fan mail, my classmates at college were very proud of me, my professors were proud of me — I just couldn't hold this inside of me, though, because I was overjoyed about being a celebrity, winning and so forth — I was overwhelmed," said Stempel. "Then Dan Enright said to me, 'You know, Herb, you're not going to get all the money you've won so far.' I said, 'What? What do you mean?' He says, 'No,' he says, 'We have to look out for ourselves, so I have a paper here which you're going to have to sign.' I realized that if I didn't sign, I wouldn't find myself on the program too much longer, so I decided to sign."[33]

Stempel stays on *Twenty-One* until the late fall of 1956, but on November 28 a more cultured, self-effacing contestant named Charles Lincoln Van Doren enters the picture. Stempel knows his days on the show are numbered, even as he and Van Doren repeatedly duel to a tie.

"I was absolutely taken aback, I was shocked, I was horrified," Stempel said. "All this celebrity business had gone to my head and I didn't want to lose, I felt that I wanted to play this game honestly, if necessary, to try to stay on. I was willing to take my chances. But Enright said 'No, you cannot do it, we've decided and you're gonna have to lose.' On the day I was to lose to Van Doren I sat at home watching television in the morning. Every few minutes an announcer would break in on WNBC saying, 'Is Herb Stempel going to win over one hundred thousand dollars tonight?' And I said, 'No, he's not going to win a hundred thousand dollars, he's going to take a dive.' "[34]

Stempel's end comes on December 5, 1956.

Stempel: "One of those questions on the final night involved the 1955 Academy Award winner. I knew that the answer was *Marty*, but Dan Enright specifically wanted me to miss that question. This hurt me very deeply because this was one of my favorite pictures of all time, and I could never forget this. A few seconds before that, as I was trying to come up with the answer, I could have changed my mind. I could have said the answer is *Marty*, instead of *On the Waterfront*, I would have won, there would be no Charles Van Doren, no famous celebrity, Charles Van Doren would have gone back to teaching college and my whole life would have been changed. . . . That evening, as had been rehearsed, I took my dive and left the program. As I walked backstage, two technicians were talking, and one said to the other one, 'At least we finally have a clean-cut intellectual on this program, not a freak with a sponge memory.' I was appalled. I was as hurt as if somebody had taken a knife and shoved it into me."[35]

***

At about the same time, something happens outside the world of *Twenty-One* and *The $64,000 Question*. Almost no one takes note, but in retrospect it signals the beginning of the end.

A lawsuit is filed in New York District Court against the producers of *The Big Surprise* by Dale Logue, a Las Vegas chorus girl who was a contestant on the show. She is seeking damages because, on air, she claims she was intentionally eliminated by being given a question she had been unable to answer during her warm-up.[36]

Variety reports: "It is claimed by her attorneys in her behalf that the 'warmup' session is a device by which contestants on quiz shows can be 'eliminated' or, conversely, by which they can be continued on the program." It's reported that Logue originally sent a letter to the producers of *The $64,000 Question* seeking consideration as a contestant, but the producers switched her to *The Big Surprise*, produced by the same company, with the promise of more money. The Federal Trade Commission takes an interest in the case. *The Big Surprise* goes off the air a few months later.[37]

***

On December 5, Stempel leaves *Twenty-One* with $49,500 and Charles Van Doren settles into a months-long stay as the champion. In the process he will become the best-known quiz contestant of the period.

Charles Van Doren, an associate professor at Columbia University, begins a 14-week run on *Twenty-One* in late 1956. He will become the best-known quiz contestant of the period.

On January 14, 1957, *Twenty-One* moves from Wednesday into the Monday timeslot on NBC that was originally going to be the home of *The Most Beautiful Girl in the World*. Now *Twenty-One* is up against *I Love Lucy*, the nation's number-one TV show since

1951. But if Lucy was once America's sweetheart, Van Doren is now. With his help, *Twenty-One* does what no regularly scheduled NBC show has done in six years: It beats *I Love Lucy* in the ratings. Van Doren receives thousands of marriage proposals in the mail, which he shyly tells Barry about on the air.[38] One note says, "I would like to meet you. I am 20, and my bust is 37."[39]

Van Doren's father, Mark, writes to his friend, the poet and Trappist monk Thomas Merton, "About fifteen million people have fallen in love with [my son] — and I don't use the word lightly."[40]

"Everybody responded to him positively," Dan Enright said. "He was the kind of guy you'd love to have your daughter married to. Attractive, likable, good sense of humor. And he just captured everyone's imagination. . . . When Van Doren was approached to appear on the program, and also told that he would be coached, his first reaction was negative. He did not want to be a part of it. And frankly we convinced him to do it by convincing him that it would help glamorize information, it would help glamorize intellectualism. His name became synonymous with quiz shows, and his impact was immediate."[41]

For TV viewers, it is as if a rather unpleasant house guest has left and a long-lost son has been welcomed home in his place. Van Doren's picture appears on the cover of *TV Guide* and *Time* — a distinction denied to his father Mark, a Pulitzer-Prize winning poet and author. (The *Time* cover breaks all records to that date for a single-issue sale.)[42]

"There are so many things I won't have to worry about now," Van Doren tells the *TV Guide* interviewer. "You know, the little things. I drive a 1948 Studebaker, and an old car traps you — can't afford to fix it and can't afford a new one. A new suit was always a problem, too. Usually, I'd just put leather patches over the elbows when a suit wore out. Now I can get that Mercedes-Benz sports car I've wanted so long, and I can buy any suit I choose."[43]

Watching Van Doren's star ascend is Herbert Stempel. As a result of bad investment advice, he has largely squandered his *Twenty-One* winnings. He goes to Dan Enright and gets some vague assurances of help.

Enright: "There was always a fear lurking that somehow the story would be exposed, that we would be revealed. And that kept gnawing at us but after a while you rationalize it and you say to yourself, 'What contestant would reveal that he played a part in the rigging?' And certainly we would never reveal that. We never took into account that a contestant might reveal his role in the rigging because he might be subjected to such trauma, and such hurt, that it would overcome whatever reluctance he had to tell the truth. . . . [Stempel was] taken from obscurity and then exposed to the light of celebrity, became for some six weeks a celebrity, and then just as quickly was cast back into obscurity. We at that time deluded ourselves into believing that what we were doing was not that wrong . . . I should have been far more mindful and far more sensitive."[44]

In 1959, *Twenty-One* producer Dan Enright will tell a congressional panel that the rigging on quiz shows is a show business tradition. Later in life, he will express remorse for the way contestant Herbert Stempel was used and discarded.

Stempel approaches a *New York Post* reporter with his story. Nothing comes of it — for the time being. Stempel also learns from Enright when Van Doren's pre-ordained fall will come, and he bets

$5,000 on his defeat. Van Doren loses, and Stempel wins $10,000, courtesy of his old nemesis.

After fourteen weeks, Van Doren's run ends on March 11, 1957, when he takes home a record $129,000 after losing to contestant Vivienne Nearing. The show draws 51.5% of the TV audience.[45]

His loss comes in an ironic way, much the same as what happened to Stempel — he muffs what is considered an "easy" question about the king of Belgium, incorrectly naming Leopold rather than his son, Baudouin.

The Associated Press, like other wire services, reports on the show as if it was a sporting event. As a publicity stunt, the government of Belgium offers Van Doren an all-expense paid trip.[46]

"All hail the new champion," Van Doren says as he emerges from the isolation booth. "I'm sure gonna have a wonderful time listening to this show next week."[47]

After 14 appearances, Charles Van Doren leaves *Twenty-One* with a record amount of cash and a dream job — to talk about whatever he wants in a regular spot on NBC's *Today* show. Once the scandal is revealed, the job doesn't last long.

As Van Doren departs, sales figures for Pharmaceuticals, Inc., the makers of Geritol, are skyrocketing in the manner of Revlon sales thanks to *The $64,000 Question* and *The $64,000 Challenge*.

The company projects 1957 revenues of $30 million — a $10 million increase over 1956. Sales of liquid Geritol are up over 70% and sales of a sleep tablet, Sominex, are up 68%.

"Television has always been successful for us," says company president Matthew Rosenhaus, "but the best return on any dollar we ever spent has been realized on *Twenty-One*."[48]

Barry and Enright start kicking around the idea of a *Twenty-One* spinoff, with a panel including past winners like Herbert Stempel and Charles Van Doren.

But Van Doren seems more interested in staying as far away from *Twenty-One* as possible. He delivers a speech to a broadcasters conference urging them to consider airing more educational programs.

"Broadcasters should have more faith in their audiences," he says, citing thousands of letters from viewers who say that, as a result of his appearances, their children are studying harder.[49]

Van Doren signs with the talent agency MCA and then goes to work for NBC-TV at ten times the salary he is making as an instructor at Columbia University.[50] He appears as a guest on *The Steve Allen Show*, moderates a news special or two and is given five minutes a day to talk about anything he wants — even seventeenth-century poetry, on which he is an expert — on Dave Garroway's *Today* show.

Van Doren is now a Television Personality, as recognized — maybe even more so — as many other performers on the tube.

From all accounts, Van Doren excelled in his role on *Today* — but watching him now on old episodes of *Twenty-One*, with the benefit of perspective, a different impression emerges: With each win, he seems more drawn, grim, preoccupied.

He seems haunted.

CHAPTER FOUR: "IT WAS A CON GAME, THAT'S ALL" (MARCH 1957-MAY 1958)

"No, the money is not of the first importance.
The first importance is that I have found friends,
great friends, among strangers. I have nothing but
words of praise and gratitude to say of the Revlon
people, who sponsor The $64,000 Question . . .
of [producers] Mr. Ben Kagan and Mr. Mert
Koplin and Mr. Hal March . . . of all the people with
whom I had the honor to be associated."
— Mrs. Frances De Berry, a $16,000 winner
on Question, *to TV-Radio Mirror, March 1957*[1]

In the spring of 1957, as *Twenty-One* rises in the ratings, *The $64,000 Question* begins a gradual slide after finishing 1956 with the most weekly finishes in first place.[2] It's usually still in the top 10, but it moves to the middle of the pack, surpassed by old favorites like *I Love Lucy* and *The Ed Sullivan Show*, or newer favorites like *The Perry Como Show*.

To goose viewer interest, a change is made regarding the amount of cash at stake — once a contestant wins $64,000, he or she can keep going to win multiples of $64,000, up to $256,000.[3]

The producers also continue their search for unique contestants — Teddy Nadler, a talkative civil service clerk who claims to have a photographic memory, wins $252,000 on *The $64,000 Question* and *The $64,000 Challenge*. Then he cheekily challenges Charles Van Doren to a quiz-off, but it's dismissed as a publicity stunt.[4]

Teddy Nadler, a civil service clerk from St. Louis, wins over $250,000 on *The $64,000 Question* and *The $64,000 Challenge*. He will later tell reporters he has a photographic memory and was never coached.

The *Question* producers find another audience favorite in ten-year-old Robert Strom of the Bronx, a fifth grader given to Brylcreemed hair and bow ties. He wins big money by working extraordinarily detailed scientific or mathematic equations — he does so on a piece of plate glass, so viewers can see it.

Pint-sized Robert Strom (shown here with his father Albert and Hal March) takes *The $64,000 Question* by storm with his expertise in mathematics and science. He will win over $250,000 on *Question* and *The $64,000 Challenge*.

In April, *Daily Variety* columnist Jack Hellman notes, "Nobody is accusing anybody of tampering with anything, but it has been inescapably noticeable how the producers of *21* are trying to build their new champ, Hank Bloomgarden, into the image of Charles Van Doren. Characteristics have been copied, the struggle within himself to remember seems to have been stenciled and the pained anguish of a fleeting thought copied. Where it worked once it won't work twice. Hank hasn't got it. The whiz kid [Robert Strom] on *$64,000 Question* has — what it takes to bring them back every week."[5]

Robert Strom does his stuff.

Strom makes the cover of *TV Guide* — the only quiz contestant, other than Charles Van Doren, to do so.

"I like all kinds of math," Strom tells the *TV Guide* interviewer. "Algebra, solid geometry, trig, calculus. I'm going to be a mathemo-physicist. That's a word I made up."

Strom's mighty intellect is contained in a small package. He stands four feet, four inches tall. In his *TV Guide* cover photo, he is being hoisted into the air by Hal March. In the article he continues:

"In school I play basketball. I'm a little short for basketball and it seems to me whenever I make a good shot the coach is looking the other way."

"Some days it doesn't pay to get up in the morning, does it?," his father said.

"It only pays on Tuesdays [the day the show airs]," said Robert.[6]

Within a few weeks there's another big winner — showgirl Barbara Hall, who is an expert on Shakespeare. She wins $64,000 on June 25 with questions read by substitute emcee Ed Sullivan, because Hal March is making a movie in Hollywood.

Hall will eventually go to Hollywood herself, change her last name to Feldon, and appear as Agent 99 on the 1960s sitcom *Get Smart*.[7]

Like Dr. Joyce Brothers, Feldon says she received no help — that, while working as a Broadway showgirl, she committed as much Shakespeare to memory as possible.

"For three months I did nothing but study Shakespeare when I got home from the show every night," Feldon told an interviewer in 2015. "I would sit cross-legged on the floor and put the book on the bed and I'd hold a sneaker in each hand and hold my arms out so that my arms would ache . . . and to overcome the pain I would, you know, study the Shakespeare things so that I wouldn't fall asleep. . . . I did get the $64,000, which I didn't even want because I was just newly poor and I was enjoying it. The last thing I wanted was wall-to-wall carpeting. I had just escaped upper middle-class Pittsburgh and here I was, [happy] in my bare-floor cold water flat."[8]

Winners are still being profiled in fan magazines, such as Mrs. De Berry (see chapter opening above) and cabdriver Thomas Kane, who says, "[T]he fare I 'picked up' on *The $64,000 Question* is the biggest I ever metered in my tallest dreams — but no dream so tall as that I would ever be looking at a checkbook, *my* checkbook, with $64,000 entered into it."[9]

And common-man contestants are still making headlines — a bible expert from Nigeria, Theophilus A. Aderonmu, withdraws from the show after revelations surface about his matrimonial status that raise the possibility of bigamy. Hal March hopes on the air that everyone involved would "become very happy."[10]

In April 1957, just a month after Charles Van Doren sets a quiz money record by winning $129,000, two more milestones are reached — on *The $64,000 Challenge*, young genius Robert Strom hits $160,000 in winnings and Teddy Nadler hits $152,000.

And what *Time* magazine calls "the $60 million question" is raised once again — are quiz shows rigged?

"From the heyday of radio's first spectacular giveaways," the article says, "quiz producers have stacked the cards to make the game as entertaining as possible. . . . [T]he producers of many shows control the outcome as closely as they dare — without collusion from contestants, yet far more effectively than viewers suspect."

As an example, the article turns to *The $64,000 Question*:

"When a contestant has reached all but the biggest payoff on *$64,000 Question*, audience psychology virtually demands his victory. In its 22 months on the air, only two of the players who elected a $64,000 question have failed to win. . . . But most big winners have been blessed by crucial questions right up their alleys. Marine Captain Richard McCutchen [sic], the cooking expert, whose particular specialty is French cuisine, got his $64,000 question in French cuisine, not in Cantonese or Neapolitan fare. Shoemaker Gino Prato, the opera expert, whose knowledge of German or French repertory is not up to his Italian specialty, got his tough questions on Italian opera. Jockey Billy Pearson, a $64,000 winner whose expertise does not extend to Chinese art, says, 'I studied like hell on Chinese art. But I never got a question on it.' "

The article concludes: "[A] kind of inflation has also hit the contestants: instead of the kind of ordinary people who struck a responsive chord in viewers, they now run to narrow specialists and photographic minds — 'freaks,' as the trade calls them. Given a margin of error for the contestants' human foibles, the producers seem to be able to control everything — except their own fears of losing their audience."[11]

At least as far as *Twenty-One* is concerned, the manipulation mentioned in the article is much more overt. And although it won't become public for another year, there's explosive evidence of that just about a month after the *Time* article appears.

On May 11, 1957, *Twenty-One* contestant James Snodgrass receives answers and instructions for his appearance on the May 13 show. He goes home and writes everything in a letter that he sends to himself via registered mail. He does the same thing on May 17, with instructions for the May 20 show.

James Snodgrass becomes a whistleblower in the quiz scandals
by writing *Twenty-One* answers he had been given in advance
and sending them to himself via registered mail.

"According to the plan," he writes in one letter, "I am to miss the first question, specifically the lines by Emily Dickinson. I've been told to answer Ralph Waldo Emerson. I have decided not to 'take the fall' but to answer the question correctly."

On the May 20 show, Snodgrass answers "Emily Dickinson," which increases his winnings to $126,000 and causes panic behind the scenes. But when objections are raised by outside medical experts over an answer Snodgrass gave to another question, it's decided that the match will be replayed on the next show. This time Snodgrass willingly loses to winner Hank Bloomgarden and ends up leaving with $4,000.

Snodgrass doesn't report his activity to anyone, but he keeps the unopened letters.

"I didn't think it was terribly wrong," he says later, "but something told me that I had better cover my ass on this."[12]

***

Herbert Stempel spends the first part of 1957 still smarting over the ascent of Charles Van Doren. He's irked when the *Time* cover story about Van Doren calls him "TV's own health-restoring antidote to (Elvis the Pelvis) Presley." He's wounded when he visits Dan Enright's office and sees a photo of Charles Van Doren in a place of honor. "[Enright] just completely forgot I ever existed," he'll say later.[13]

Stempel is walking a fine line — he has talked to a reporter at the *New York Post* about the rigging but he's also trying to stay in the good graces of Jack Barry and Dan Enright. They keep talking about their planned *Twenty-One* spinoff and they keep tempting Stempel with the promise of becoming a regular. But Stempel needs cash now — he admits to Enright that he has "piddled away" most of his earnings. He keeps raising the possibility of blackmail, but, again, doesn't want to risk killing the golden goose.

Enright, sensing that something is up, finally produces a statement denying any rigging on *Twenty-One* and gives it to Stempel to sign.

The statement reads: "I do hereby state and declare to whomever may be now or in the future concerned that Dan Enright, producer of Barry & Enright Productions, has never in any way, shape nor form given, imparted or suggested to me any questions or answers connected with the program *21*."

It's a lie, of course. But, although it will return to haunt him, Stempel signs it, fearing that if he doesn't he won't be on the new panel show.

Then in late March, NBC buys out Barry and Enright. Reports *Variety*: "[It's] a deal reporting reaching seven figures and which, though the exact amount has been kept under wraps, elevates partners Jack Barry and Dan Enright into 'very rich' brackets." The amount is later reported to be over $2 million.[14]

Talk of any *Twenty-One* spinoff begins to dry up, and Stempel again begins reaching out to anyone who'll listen.

In 1992, the principals involved told their stories on a PBS documentary:

Stempel: "I . . . contacted Jack O'Brien, who was a columnist for the *Journal-American* who covered television, and I told him the story. He believed me, but he . . . would never come out directly and accuse them of perpetrating a hoax on the people."

O'Brien: "Ultimately one day I get a phone call for the *Journal-American* and the chief operator said there was a fellow named Herb Stempel wanted to talk to me. We talked for four hours! At first I thought it might be a crank, I thought it might be a phony, but everything hung together in his story."

Enright: "Sure enough, within two days I received a phone call from a newspaper, saying that they had been advised by a contestant who had appeared on the show that the show was rigged. I asked him if that person was Herb Stempel and they said yes it was."

O'Brien: "We could never get it printed in flat factual terms because the lawyers for my newspaper syndicate wouldn't touch it until we had absolute proof."[15]

***

At about this same time, a minister from Tullahoma, Tennessee named Charles E. "Stoney" Jackson writes to the producers of *The*

$64,000 Question. He has an entrepreneurial bent, and he is trying to start a series of football "Christian Bowls," merging religion with high school football. To raise money for the project, and a projected boys' home, Jackson suggests appearing on the show as an expert in sports or boxing.

The Rev. Charles "Stoney" Jackson goes on *The $64,000 Question* and *The $64,000 Challenge* to fund "Christian Bowls" for high school football teams. Along with Herbert Stempel, he will be one of the first quiz whistleblowers. "The scandals," he will say later, "started me on the road to cynicism."

He gets a call from a show producer, telling him he needs to choose a more attention-getting category.

So he responds that his expertise is in "Great Lovers" — even though, he says later, his recent failed marriage was "a great recommendation for celibacy."[16] The producers suggest it be changed to "Great Love Stories" and they bring Jackson to New York.

In a conference with producer Mert Koplin before going on the show, Jackson begins to get the funny feeling that it is a rehearsal more than a meeting. After winning his first round by answering a question that came up before the show, Jackson goes home to Tullahoma for a week. He confesses his unease to a fellow minister who advises him not to worry. Jackson returns to New York and appears several more times on *Question* — after he wins $8,000, he tells Hal March that he is in "hog heaven." He then works his way up to winning $16,000. And by that point it is strongly indicated to him that he needs to take the money rather than try for $32,000.[17]

He later recalled the words of a production assistant on the show: "I hope you don't make the mistake another contestant did when he ignored the signal and decided to go on anyway. He was given a question they knew he couldn't handle, and he lost." (This description fits contestant Al Einfrank, a truck driver and expert at geography who tried for $32,000 and missed, lost the $16,000 he had won to that point, and ended up with a Cadillac convertible valued at about $5,000.)[18]

Jackson takes the hint, stops at $16,000, and goes back to Tennessee with his winnings, but he will return to New York — and to television — very soon.

***

Without question, Stoney Jackson and Herbert Stempel are the two squeaky wheels who helped bring an end to the era of rigged quizzes. They're a pair of contrasts — Stempel is stocky, Jewish, a nerdy urbanite, while Jackson is a lanky Disciples of Christ minister from the small-town South. Stempel loves movies and classic literature. Jackson loves sports — both participating in them and using them as a way to save souls. But they are both garrulous types, never turning down an interview, each living in modest to lower-class settings. (When Jackson is interviewed by *Los Angeles Times* TV columnist Howard Rosenberg in 1989, he is penniless and living in Denver.)

The biggest thing they had in common was the resolve to expose a crooked system, but their motives were different — Jackson claimed to want to right a wrong. Stempel wanted revenge on

Van Doren and the Ivy League background he represented. If they both became celebrities in the process, that would be the cherry on top of the sundae.

***

In August comes another article with questions about quiz shows, this time in *Look* magazine.

The article says: "With quiz shows a national mania (in 1956, almost $5,500,000 was given away in prizes), fans are wondering just how they work. They want to know whether shows are fixed, particularly whether contestants are asked questions it is known they can answer . . . Most quiz-show producers dismiss inquiries about 'fixes' curtly, but such an attitude, no matter how sincere, has failed to satisfy even the TV critics. Harriet Van Horne of the New York *World-Telegram* scoffs at such 'pious' innocence and reminds viewers of Ralph Waldo Emerson's remark: 'The louder he talked of his honor, the faster we counted our spoons!' Obviously, the skeptics will not be easily silenced. They want proof. . . . No TV quiz shows are fixed in the sense of being dishonest. It may be more accurate to say that they are controlled or partially controlled."[19]

***

As 1957 comes to an end, Stoney Jackson returns to New York City to appear on *The $64,000 Challenge*.

"I came to New York for the *Challenge*, " Jackson told an interviewer in the early 1990s. "And the producer? Her name was Shirley Bernstein. She was the sister of Leonard Bernstein. I was in the office, she looked at me and said, 'Do you know who wrote a poem similar to Marlowe's on Hero and Leander?' I said, 'No, I do not.' As I walked out of the office, she yelled at me, 'It was Thomas Hood.' And in that [isolation] booth, I was totally surprised when the question turned out to be [about] Thomas Hood. There was the temptation to say to [emcee] Ralph Story, 'I know the answer to this because Shirley Bernstein gave it to me.' It was a con game, that's all. A scam, from start to finish."[20]

Jackson wins $4,000 — out of guilt he shares some of it with the contestant he'd defeated. Then he reaches out to *Time* magazine, *The New York Times*, and the Nashville *Tennessean*.[21] No response. And Jackson soon finds himself ostracized by the people of Tullahoma for his outspokenness. (That animus continued for decades, at least according to my personal experience. In the early 1990s I found myself in Tullahoma visiting my wife's relatives. I had just read Howard Rosenberg's interview with Jackson and was intrigued. I asked if anyone there had ever known Stoney Jackson. They had, and their unanimous response, in so many words: "He was a nut.")

By early 1958, quiz shows — and quiz-show winners — are making news less often. Audiences are warming to another genre of TV show — the newer "adult" western, as opposed to older western shoot-em-ups aimed at kids, with stars like Roy Rogers or William "Hopalong Cassidy" Boyd.

In January, Revlon lets it be known that it's ready to drop its co-sponsorship of *The $64,000 Challenge*.[22] And in February, when the ARB ratings service lists the month's top 25 primetime TV programs, the *$64,000* shows and *Twenty-One* are nowhere to be seen, crowded out by "adult" westerns *Gunsmoke*, *Maverick*, *Wagon Train*, and *Have Gun, Will Travel*. (23)

In March 1958, Lou Cowan, anointed a programming genius because of *The $64,000 Question*, is promoted from vice-president to president of CBS Television.

Variety writes: "As creator of such successful program entries as *The $64,000 Question* and its companion *The $64,000 Challenge* (plus such previous toprated [sic] shows as *Stop the Music*), Cowan's primary area has been programming, but during his tenure as staff veepee he has been shuttling around in all areas of the company."[24]

Meanwhile, over at Revlon, brothers Martin and Charles Revson are feuding. In *Sponsor* magazine, columnist Joe Csida writes:

"I have a number of friends involved with one or another of the television packages Revlon has purchased. . . . Even in comparatively serene days, say these pals, the Revlon operation is a soul-tester. But in recent months, with the battle between president Charles Revson and his executive vice president brother Martin coming to a head, it has been a situation to wrench sobs from a Spartan. . . . Before Martin quit or was fired or was bought out of the Revlon empire they were making and selling about 30 different products. . . . Revlon had five agencies handing the various products . . . no agency man, advertiser or broadcaster need know more than a few simple, basic facts about the Revlon beauty trust to appreciate the behind-the-scenes potential for ulcers of previously unheard-of dimensions."[25]

Joseph Stone, the assistant district attorney who would soon be guiding the grand jury probe into quiz shows, told Jeff Kisseloff, "When we were investigating the quiz shows, Martin Revson, who was really second fiddle in Revlon, told me that he and his brother were continually at each other's throats. One Friday they had a terrible row. Martin stormed out of his office. When he returned Monday, his office was gone. Everything on the walls, his furniture. Gone."[26]

In a suit filed in 1960, Martin Revson will claim that "Charles Revson engaged in a practice of mistreating executives of Revlon, Inc. and abusing them personally to such extent that men of proven capacity who held high positions in nationally known corporations before and after their employment by Revlon, Inc. suffered humiliation and impaired efficiency and left Revlon, Inc. to escape mistreatment."[27]

Adds *Time* magazine: "To underlings and admen who do not know them [sic], Revson is a relentless taskmaster. He has axed his way through seven different ad agencies in the past three years, rubbed off dozens of account executives. At one time his executive turnover was so great that people who stayed at Revlon a year, so the story goes, got together and had an oldtimers' lunch."[28]

As the summer of 1958 begins, Revlon is reviewing its options for the upcoming TV season. It looks like *The $64,000 Challenge* will move to NBC, with Revlon out as a sponsor. *The $64,000 Question* is losing its Tuesday night timeslot to Garry Moore's new variety show, so *Question* will be moved into the Sunday night spot on CBS once occupied by *Challenge*.

There's also a new daytime quiz show called *Dotto* that gains some notice — so much so that soon the sponsor, Colgate-Palmolive, adds a nighttime version.

Says *Broadcasting* magazine in a review:

"*Dotto* is the Chevrolet of quiz shows. Streamlined and quick-moving, it is not so expensive as *Twenty-One* (the Cadillac of the quizzes) nor so intellectual as *The $64,000 Question* (the Jaguar). Rather, it whizzes through 30 minutes of questions, dashboard gimmicks, contestants and emceeing calculated to entertain the mass audience. . . . The program derives its name from large pictures formed by dots which are joined as the contestants answer elementary school questions correctly. Everybody seems to enjoy himself tremendously, particularly the audience, which sounds like a fight crowd at Madison Square Garden."[29]

No one realizes it at the time, but *Dotto* is doomed to a short life. And the cheering crowd is about to turn ugly.

CHAPTER FIVE: "THESE QUIZ SHOWS ARE DRIVING US CRAZY" (MAY 1958-JUNE 1959)

"Bing Crosby—Barry Fitzgerald—Abbie [sic] Players—
Donald Duck-3 nephews—
Dagwood—Mr. Dithers"
— answers scrawled in a notebook by Dotto
contestant Marie Winn just before
she utters them on the air

May 20, 1958: Edward Hilgemeier Jr., an aspiring actor-comic and occasional butler-bartender, is hoping to make a few bucks when he walks into a New York TV studio to appear as a contestant on daytime *Dotto*. He's been appearing sporadically as a contestant on various quiz shows for about six months, going so far as to win $3,000 worth of merchandise on *The Price Is Right*.[1]

Today Hilgemeier is a standby contestant, which means he probably won't appear on the air, but he has to show up at the studio just in case his match begins earlier than expected.

In the same room sits Marie Winn, a young woman who is appearing on that day's *Dotto*. Hilgemeier doesn't find her very friendly — she spends most of her time before the broadcast hunched over a notebook, explaining that she's studying for her exams at Columbia.[2]

At air time, Winn goes before the cameras and begins playing *Dotto*, a game where contestants stand at podiums decorated with the sponsor's products — in this case, Colgate toothpaste or Ajax cleanser — and answer questions. Each correct answer is worth a dot; gradually. the dots are connected to reveal the face of a famous person. Hilgemeier watches the show on a TV monitor. Curious at the ease with which Winn answers her questions, Hilgemeier grabs the notebook she's left behind and looks inside.

On one page are the answers that, just at that moment, Winn is giving on the air.

After the show, Hilgemeier and Yeffe Kimball Slatin, the contestant whom Winn has just defeated, approach the *Dotto* producers with their evidence and the threat of exposure. But they aren't interested in righting a wrong — they're interested in a payoff to keep their mouths shut. They hire an attorney to negotiate cash settlements for each of them. A few days later, unbeknownst to Hilgemeier, Slatin receives $4,000. Hilgemeier hires another attorney and keeps negotiating for his hush money.

He also reaches out to reporter Jack O'Grady at the *New York Post,* who tells Hilgemeier that the story needs a "peg" beyond just the accusations of an angry contestant. File a complaint with the FCC, O'Grady tells Hilgemeier. *That* will make it a story. O'Grady even helps him write it. He also advises Hilgemeier to take the $1,500 settlement that's being offered to him, and the *Post* will pay an additional $500.

In early August, believing the affidavit is still in O'Grady's hands and has not yet been submitted to the FCC, Hilgemeier goes to the Colgate-Palmolive offices on Park Avenue. Hilgemeier tells company executives that he believes he's being blacklisted as a result of his whistle-blowing, and proposes a deal — if Colgate promises to help him, and gives him another $2,500 so his settlement will be the same amount as Slatin's, he won't file the affidavit.[3]

Then Hilgemeier finds out that he doesn't have any leverage over Colgate because O'Grady has already filed the affidavit. On Monday, August 18, O'Grady's story hits the *Post,* headlined: "Next Question: Why Did *Dotto* Die?" That same morning, viewers expecting to see *Dotto* on CBS are informed that the show has been abruptly cancelled.

The next day, *The New York Times* reports the cancellation. Just below the news item is a story describing the previous night's wins and losses on *Twenty-One*.[4]

Reports *Variety*: "*Dotto* has gone blotto . . . with virtually everyone involved, including network officials, the sponsor, advertising agency, et. al. clamming up tighter than an atomic scientist. . . . The *Dotto* case isn't the first time that someone accused a quiz of being rigged, but it was the first time that the accusation was put in the form of an affidavit. . . . Crux of the situation is that henceforth charges against quizzes will be rampant. Worse, the hypersensitive ad agencies are expected to give credence to each and every gripe in return."[5]

Jack Narz, the host of *Dotto*, is not implicated in the rigging of the show. He tells a reporter, "They asked me if I knew what had happened, and I said no. They said 'Good, let's keep it that way.' " Narz will go on to host a long line of game shows, including *Concentration*, *Now You See It*, and *Beat the Clock*.

In the wake of the cancellation, syndicated columnist Dick Kleiner interviews the show's emcee, Jack Narz." I'm still in a state of shock," he says. "I still haven't been told the whole story, just that my contract was cancelled. They asked me if I knew what had happened. I said no. They said, 'Good, let's keep it that way.' "[6]

Based on Hilgemeier's story, New York City Assistant District Attorney Joseph Stone, a specialist in prosecuting fraud, begins an investigation of *Dotto*. The ensuing probe, including a grand jury, will stretch over the course of more than a year.

***

Hilgemeier becomes a momentary media celebrity.

"People tell me I might have come off better if I hadn't accepted the $1,500," Hilgemeier tells *New York Herald Tribune* TV columnist Marie Torre. "Well, I don't know. I really have no regrets I did what I did."[7]

"Since the TV schedule now devotes 78 half hours each week to quiz shows — an investment of some 24 million dollars — the ultimate consequences of Hilgemeier's cry of dirty pool could be fairly stupendous," writes TV columnist Harriet Van Horne.[8] "The enormous cash prizes and dream-world merchandise . . . may become a thing of the past. Such quizzes as survive may go back to giving $100 savings bonds and pop-up toasters."

There are reports that Stone's probe is expanding — that he and his team have begun questioning other *Dotto* contestants, as well as network and production executives.

"The D.A.'s office, it was reported, also received squawks regarding the behavior pattern of other quiz shows on the networks," reports *Variety*.[9]

Squawking the loudest, as soon as he hears about the case, is Herbert Stempel.

Stempel: "I picked up a copy of a newspaper and read in there that [they were] planning to launch a probe about quiz shows. This was after the *Dotto* scandal had broken, and I went to a telephone booth — I remember this as if it happened yesterday — [and] made a call to the district attorney's office."[10]

Stempel also calls the newspapers. And on August 28, as Stempel is talking to ADA Joseph Stone, The New York *Journal-American* and the New York *World-Telegram & Sun* both carry Stempel's story.

Stone: "I interviewed Stempel over a period of about five days. It was very interesting because I really almost didn't have to keep notes about what Stempel told me — all I had to do was buy a newspaper and there was a story. He had told the story to the *Journal-American* and they had complete notes of what he told them, so this is what they published."[11]

Stempel spends more than 12 hours telling his story to Stone.[12] In response to Stempel's allegations, *Twenty-One* co-producers Barry and Enright file a libel suit against the *World-Telegram*. They go on to deny any wrongdoing and release the false statement signed by Stempel on March 7, 1957, disavowing receiving any help.

In a dramatic press conference a few days later, Enright says that in early 1957, after he left *Twenty-One*, Stempel threatened to claim that the show was rigged unless he got some cash. Barry and Enright then play a tape recording of the March 7 meeting between Enright and Stempel. On it, Stempel answers "yes" to Enright's assertion of blackmail. Barry and Enright also strongly infer that Stempel is unbalanced and needs psychiatric treatment. Stempel claims the tape is doctored.[13]

"I never attempted blackmail," Stempel says. "I've never confessed to anything except that *Twenty-One* was fixed."[14]

"I was a damn fool to have signed such a thing, to have agreed to such a thing," Stempel says later, "but they then held out the prospects of money, of jobs, and this and that, to me, and I succumbed to that."[15]

On September 8, Jack Barry opens *Twenty-One* with a statement: "Before the program starts there is something I must say to all of you. I am talking about the stories that you have read attacking my partner, Dan Enright, and me. All I want to say is this: The stories are wholly untrue. I repeat, they are wholly untrue. At no time has any contestant ever been given advance information about any questions ever used on this program. It has been a terrible experience to have to combat the unfounded charges that have been flying at us, but we do consider ourselves lucky in one respect. So many of you have expressed your faith in us and in our program. A wise man once said the truth will win out. I know that it will for we have not betrayed your trust in us. We never will."[16]

By now, the district attorney's office is regularly quizzing contestants and staff members from *Twenty-One* and *Dotto*.

A *Dotto* winner, Regan Leydenfrost, agrees to talk to reporters after her meeting with Stone. She says that although she wasn't given exact answers to questions, "Anyone would have been an idiot not to have been able to give the answers" based on the information she was given.[17]

As the scope of the inquiry broadens, Charles Van Doren is asked for a statement.

He responds: "I never got any kind of a hint or help, and, as far as I know, nobody ever did on the program. I have heard rumors of irregularities on quiz shows, but I never have heard any proof. Most of the shows are absolutely on the up-and-up."[18]

Now it's Stoney Jackson's turn to speak up about his experiences on *The $64,000 Challenge*, although he adds that he saw no collusion on *The $64,000 Question*.[19]

In *Daily Variety*, a spokesman for the co-sponsor of *Challenge*, tobacco company P. Lorillard, says the client is "greatly disturbed over the unfavorable publicity."[20]

Although no one knows it at the time, the episode of *The $64.000 Challenge* that airs the night after Jackson's story hits the wires is the final episode. On September 12, the P. Lorillard tobacco company drops its sponsorship, and the planned switch of the show to NBC is scrapped. Lorillard officials decide to back another type of TV program — no more quiz shows.

Bad omens are in the air.

On September 9, a door sticks on the isolation booth used on the ABC game show *Who Do You Trust?* and traps a contestant inside for twelve minutes during a live broadcast.[21]

On September 15, reports *The New York Times*, "a network news executive took note of the fast-breaking developments . . . and commented, 'These quiz shows are driving us crazy.' "[22]

The emerging scandal is also fodder for comedians — on *The Tonight Show* Jack Paar jokes about playing "Honest Dotto"[23] and Bob Hope offers several one-liners:

"Remember 21? Now it's 30-to-life. No wonder those quiz shows give away all that dough — they need it for bail! There's been more singing on Dotto *than on the* Hit Parade."[24]

On his radio show, comic Jack Carson asks, "Anyone want to buy 10 unconnected dots?"[25]

The president of ABC Television, Oliver Treyz, also scores with his own zinger. Because the network has virtually no big-money quiz shows on its schedule, Treyz tells a group of ABC affiliates, "The only fixed shows we have are the westerns."[26]

Meanwhile Herbert Stempel, back in the media spotlight, makes his own splash in a national magazine — in its September 15 issue, *Life* features photos of Stempel demonstrating the various expressions — deep thought, anxiety, triumph — that he says he was coached on during his *Twenty-One* stint.

"The public," the article says, "was learning that what it assumed to be bright, clean fun was perhaps not so bright or as clean as it looked."[27]

In *Broadcasting* magazine, Joseph Cates, one-time producer of *The $64,000 Question*, steadfastly defends the honor of the quiz show despite the emerging facts.

"People in our business are like everybody else," he says. "We're basically honest. There are a few quacks in every business, and no doubt we have our share. But I don't think we have more than our share; most of us are honest. . . . If this investigation has been able to turn up only a handful of contestants crying 'fix,' out of all the thousands of contestants who've been on these shows, then you can be sure the shows have been fundamentally honest."[28]

***

Since beginning his investigation in late August, ADA Joseph Stone and his staff have interviewed people associated with *Dotto* and *Twenty-One*, including contestants, producers, and attorneys representing producers and television networks.

There's plenty of shadiness to go around. But is any of it illegal?

It's a question the DA's office struggles with. The shows were never listed as bonafide sporting contests, so there is no fraud. No one was swindled out of any money — on the contrary, contestants were well paid for taking a dive.

Stone would later write:

"[District Attorney Frank] Hogan asked if I was really convinced we should continue with the investigation. It was a very serious question. With show business involved, the scandal promised to be a continuing sensation in the press. As such, it offered to an ambitious district attorney — or for that matter, an ambitious assistant district attorney — considerable temptations. On the other hand, a single mistake could mean being eaten alive by the press and damage our office's reputation for professionalism. But the can of worms was already open — to drop the investigation could provoke cries of cover-up or special treatment. . . . I told Hogan I believed we had no choice but to follow the investigation through and see whether we were being made fools of or were on the track of a major crime."[29]

On September 12, DA Hogan announces that there will be a grand jury probe of quiz shows.

"Charges and countercharges have been made against individuals and businesses and have received a great deal of publicity," Hogan says. He adds that is "not a fair assumption that we have concluded that there has been wrongdoing."[30]

On September 17, 1958, Stone convenes a twenty-three member grand jury in lower Manhattan and begins listening to over one hundred people testify on whether TV quiz shows are rigged.

Later, the District Attorney's office will estimate that three-quarters of them lied under oath.

Producers lie about orchestrating matches and rigging outcomes. Production assistants lie about feeding answers to contestants before a broadcast, or about tailoring questions to fit a contestant's knowledge. Some of the contestants themselves lie about getting help before going on the air.

Stone later wrote, "The great mystery became for my associates and me not how or why the shows were fixed — this emerged early in the investigation — but why so many people were willing to break the law by lying about an activity, quiz rigging, which, when they were engaged in it, was not illegal, even after we advised them of that fact."[31]

The grand jury is presided over by General Sessions Judge Mitchell Schweitzer, who reminds the jurors that grand jury proceedings are secret — the jurors are not to reveal to anybody anything of their discussion or how they voted individually on any matter. No testimony of any witness can be disclosed except by order of the court. He further explains that Stone and his team will serve as the jury's legal advisers in charge of the presentation of the evidence.[32]

The next day, September 18, jurors begin hearing from witnesses connected with *Dotto*, including Edward Hilgemeier, Yeffe Slatin and a dozen other contestants.

They also hear from *Dotto* producer Edward Jurist, who defends the control of quiz shows.

"You cannot ask random questions of people and have a show," Jurist says. "You simply have failure, failure, failure, and that does not make entertainment." He describes the importance of the show's "plot" — how, after every broadcast, he and his associates would determine what would happen tomorrow, taking in the opinions of the agency and sponsor.[33]

The jury then turns to *Twenty-One* as former contestants are brought in for questioning. Dairy farmer Harold Craig, the winner of $106,000, admits that he was coached and told when to take the fall.[34] Rose Leibbrand, the president of a women's professional organization, tells of appearing on *Twenty-One* in the hopes of generating publicity for her group, but is abruptly told to lose to then-champion Herbert Stempel.[35] Hank Bloomgarden, who won $98,500, says no coaching was involved in his wins, but will later recant.[36]

Some of the most dramatic evidence comes from James Snodgrass, who appeared on *Twenty-One* in 1957. He produces the registered letters he mailed to himself (see Chapter Four), proving rigging, and opens them for the first time in front of the grand jury.

The testimony of Craig, Leibbrand, Bloomgarden and Snodgrass reveals one common thread — the direct involvement of *Twenty-One* producer Albert Freedman in the rigging. But when questioned under oath, Freedman denies everything. So on November 7, Freedman is indicted by the grand jury for perjury.[37]

At a press conference, DA Hogan is asked if Freedman specifically coached contestants Stempel or Snodgrass. Hogan can't name names but when asked how many contestants, Hogan replies: "Plural. I'll stick to plural."[38]

If the fall of 1955 was the glorious dawn of the big-money quiz era, heralded by the meteoric rise of *The $64,000 Question*, then the fall of 1958 is the ominous dusk.

In September, a work of fiction called *The Hot Half Hour* is published. Its author, Robert L. Foreman, is a former advertising man whose clients included Revlon. In the book, an advertising agency executive tells the producer of a hit quiz show: "You've control over the questions, the contestants, the timing, the spacing of the contestants, and, therefore, as complete control over the results as does the director of a dramatic show."

The book continues: "[The producer] agreed to put the boy on the following week, and then had to get rid of the little girl though we'd been planning on her for weeks more. A real curve of a question, specially prepared, and it was goodbye to the kid."[39]

At NBC, production of the Barry & Enright quizzes — including *Twenty-One, Tic Tac Dough* and *Dough Re Mi* — is taken over by the network. Barry and Enright claim they asked NBC to take over so they can devote their energies to "disproving the unfounded charges against the integrity" of their shows.[40] DA Frank Hogan reports that his office is receiving more mail about the quiz show probe than on any case he can remember, with about 75% of the letters criticizing the quizzers.[41]

In addition, the once-mighty quiz shows are getting pummeled in the ratings, with *Twenty-One* running a distant second to the ABC sitcom *The Real McCoys*,[42] and *The $64,000 Question*, in its new Sunday-night slot, far behind the Loretta Young anthology series on NBC.[43]

Between the negative publicity and the bad ratings, something's gotta give. On October 16, *Twenty-One* is cancelled[44] and *The $64,000 Question* bites the dust on November 2. It is reported that during its three-and-a-half-year run, *Question* gave away $2.1 million in cash and 29 Cadillac convertibles as consolation prizes. CBS executive vice president Hubbell Robinson Jr. says: "Although the integrity of the first . . . big quiz show was not an issue in the replacement, *The $64,000 Question* has nevertheless become a victim of declining quiz show audiences."

Adds the article: "Mr. Robinson did not explain his reference to 'integrity,' but apparently he alluded to a current investigation into practices of certain quiz shows by the office of District Attorney Frank S. Hogan."[45]

And while it's true that Stone's team and the grand jury haven't been focusing on *The $64,000 Question* or *The $64,000 Challenge*, that is about to change.

***

The probe of the *$64,000* quiz shows involves celebrity contestants as well as regular ones.

Celebrities like bandleader Xavier Cugat indignantly refuse to admit they received any help. So does young actress Patty Duke who appears on *The $64,000 Challenge* with another young actor, Eddie Hodges, to answer questions about popular music.

Cugat will later acknowledge he was given answers, as will Duke.[46]

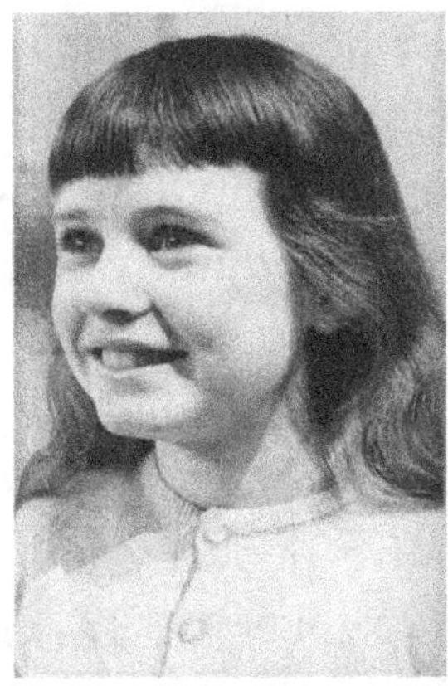

Young actress Patty Duke will reluctantly reveal that she was coached and given the answers in advance on *The $64,000 Challenge.* Soon after, she achieves fame as the star of *The Miracle Worker* on Broadway and in Hollywood.

After interviews with Eddie Hodges and Dr. Joyce Brothers, Stone comes to the conclusion that they are telling the truth — they weren't directly coached.

Stone later writes, "[The producers] relied on contestants with genuine knowledge of their subjects, and determined this by careful screening. This factor made for the significant difference between the $64,000 shows and other quizzes — only in emergencies did the producers need the contestants' direct collusion in order to rig the outcomes."[47]

On October 10, Stone and his team interview young Robert Strom, the whiz kid who has won a total of $224,000 on *Question* and *Challenge*. Stone doesn't believe that Strom was coached, but nevertheless Strom's father angrily reaches out to the *New York Post*. On October 12 there's a story headlined "Dad Terms DA's Call of Boy Quiz Whiz 'a Shame.' " Albert Strom tells the paper that those who had "no unfortunate experience on quiz shows should not be subject to the investigation."[48]

Two executives associated with *The $64,000 Question* willingly cooperate with the probe — producer Mert Koplin and Revlon marketing manager George Abrams.

Koplin describes in detail a process he calls "playback," where a contestant's responses to a series of questions helps outline his or her scope of knowledge. He tells the jury that "playback" was behind the success of the show's first $64,000 winner, Capt, Richard McCutcheon — that Koplin wrote only questions that he knew McCutcheon could answer.

Stone writes: "Asked if he thought the public would have watched if it had known the contestants were being helped, Koplin said he could not answer, but he was certain that his shows had entertained, stimulated, and challenged the public while avoiding violence and bloodshed. He cited the letters of praise and appreciation [the producers] had received from educational institutions whose enrollments had increased and teachers whose students were working harder, in direct response to the shows. 'Deceitful?' he asked back. 'Not at all. This was great entertainment for all.' "[49]

George Abrams described the weekly meetings at Revlon after each show, including Charles and Martin Revson and *Question* executives Harry Fleischman, Steve Carlin and Joseph Cates.

Stone writes: "A true believer that the power of advertising makes life better for all, Abrams was no fool, and outspoken about the foolishness of others. . . . [He said that at the meetings] every aspect of the most recent and upcoming broadcasts was evaluated. . . . Abrams conceded that this degree of personal involvement by a sponsor's top executives in the so-called creative control of a program was unusual, but the Revsons were unusual and the program was a gold mine."[50]

The grand jury also hears from Shirley Bernstein, the production assistant accused of coaching by Stoney Jackson on *The $64,000 Challenge*. Bernstein admits her involvement with Jackson, as well as with young performers Patty Duke and Eddie Hodges. She tells the investigators: "No one wants children to lose. If they missed they would be hurt at school with their playmates, their parents. If you were going to have children on the show — all I handled had good to superior knowledge — they must not be hurt in any way. . . . It was my policy and I was never contradicted in it."[51]

Bernstein also confirms at least one instance of outright rigging, involving a contestant named Wilton Springer. After winning $8,000 on *The $64,000 Question* by answering questions in the theatre category, Springer goes on *The $64,000 Challenge* and competes against another theatre buff named Arthur Cohn. The plan is for Springer to win — he's a mild-mannered working stiff (a door-to-door salesman) whose love of theatre is similar to cobbler Gino Prato's passion for opera.

Before the show, Bernstein prepares Springer by asking him questions that will appear on the air. Springer then tells Cohn about the questions he was asked in the prep session. When Cohn hears the same questions being read on the air to Springer, he gets angry and threatens to sue, but the threat never comes to pass.[52]

Some members of the grand jury want to question the man behind *The $64,000 Question* — Louis Cowan, now president of CBS Television.

Stone demurs.

"We had no evidence that Cowan was personally involved in rigging the *Question* and *Challenge*; even if there were something phony about Cowan's public stance over the years about what he tried to accomplish with his shows, there was nothing remotely illegal about it."[53]

***

By November the grand jury is back to interviewing former *Twenty-One* contestants. One is Elfrida Von Nardroff, who appeared on the show 21 times and left with $220,500. She has already told Stone that her winnings on the show were the result of extensive study, that she filled dozens of notebooks with information and haunted the New York Public Library. Appearing before the grand jury, she brings in only four notebooks, only partially filled. She is questioned about the inconsistencies in her story, and about her frequent phone calls to *Twenty-One* producer Albert Freedman, now indicted for perjury.[54]

Another contestant called before the grand jury is Vivienne Nearing, the woman who defeated Charles Van Doren. An attorney, she denies having received assistance, but when she is presented with a copy of a check from the producers for $10,000, she admits that the amount was payment for agreeing to stay on the show for several weeks while audience interest was still high.[55]

On *Twenty-One*, Charles Van Doren's downfall comes
at the hands of Vivienne Nearing in March 1957.

On January 13, Charles Van Doren appears before the grand jury for the first time after being questioned in private by Stone and his staff. He is given eight sets of questions he was asked on *Twenty-One* and misses the same questions he missed on the air.[56]

The grand jury also conducts probes into controlled quiz shows such as *Name That Tune* and *Tic Tac Dough*. Although the contestants aren't household names like Gino Prato or Charles Van Doren, they were also welcomed into millions of households each week.

One of them is U.S. Army Captain Michael O'Rourke, who won $108,500 on *Tic Tac Dough*, another show produced by Barry & Enright.

Another is John Glenn, future astronaut and U.S. Senator. He won $25,000 on *Name That Tune* as part of a team with young actor Eddie Hodges.

Hodges is a minor celebrity — he's appearing on Broadway in *The Music Man*. His expertise is popular music, and he goes from *Name That Tune* to *The $64,000 Challenge* as an expert in that category.

In the course of his investigation, Stone comes to believe that, like Hodges, Glenn wasn't overtly coached. He's not as certain regarding O'Rourke.

***

In April, Albert Freedman tells Stone that he wants to appear before the grand jury and recant his testimony. He admits giving assistance to Charles Van Doren, Hank Bloomgarden, James Snodgrass, Harold Craig and Elfrida Von Nardroff, among others. He denies helping Nearing, and also denies that he's only protecting her so she isn't disbarred. He leaves open the possibility that someone else could have helped her.[57]

Nine months after it began, the grand jury ends its work by preparing a report, or presentment.

Without naming names of any truthful contestants, the present-ment nonetheless harshly criticizes the producers of the quiz shows who rationalized that the programs were only "entertainment" and skewers them for including children in their rigging. It also argues that although the practices broke no laws, the rigging violated "social codes," manipulated people into lying and other deceitful behavior, and ruined the reputations of many.[58]

Stone senses that, for some reason, Judge Mitchell Schweitzer seems lukewarm to the idea of releasing the presentment. Stone's suspicions are confirmed when he and a group of jurors meet with the judge in late April 1959:

"[Schweitzer] had come to the conclusion, he announced, that the presentment would not be legal, therefore he could not accept it for filing and publication. . . . I had heard all this before, but it was the first formal expression of Schweitzer's attitude to the jurors, who were furious at the prospect of having the fruit of their long labor plucked from them."[59]

Stone and jury foreman Louis Hacker argue forcefully for the release of the grand jury's report — covering 59 jury sessions and over 200 interviews with 150 witnesses. But in a virtually unprece-dented action, Schweitzer orders it sealed, amid rumors that he is being pressured to do so by one — or even several — high-powered game-show producers.[60]

On June 10, Stone tells the press: "The community owes the grand jury a vote of gratitude. It has uprooted a tawdry hoax which was perpetuated on the American public. It is hopeful that its report will have a salutary effect on certain segments of the television industry."[61]

Hacker is outraged about the sealing. "Even though we're dis-charged," he tells reporters, "we cannot discuss the contents [of the report] because we're still under the jurisdiction of the court. The members of the grand jury knew that our business is super-secret — that nobody is supposed to know what a grand jury is going to do. Ask Judge Schweitzer who challenged the presentment and who knew it was to be handed up."[62]

Responds Schweitzer: "I don' t know what Mr. Hacker is talking about."[63]

CHAPTER SIX: "WE PLAYED THE WHOLE THING LIKE A SOLEMN MINUET" (JUNE-OCTOBER 1959)

"He came and said he had told the [New York] Post reporter all about this . . . at which point, instead of punching him in the nose, we gave him $1,500." — Dotto *producer Ed Jurist on paying off whistleblower Edward Hilgemeier, testifying in Washington, 1959*[1]

As the summer of 1959 progresses, ADA Joseph Stone and grand jury foreman Louis Hacker continue their efforts to overturn the sealing of the grand jury's presentment by judge Mitchell Schweitzer.

"Hitherto," wrote Stone, "the procedure invariably followed was that the court received and disclosed the contents of a presentment. Anyone who desired to have the report quashed moved in court for expungement of the offending part or whole, and the court then made a decision. But Schweitzer had sealed the quiz presentment before anyone with a possible objection had the opportunity to read it."[2]

Stone's memo to the judge asking him to reconsider his order argues that the presentment addresses a public concern, that the vast majority of presentments are made public, and that the report names no names.

***

Then on July 5, Stone flies to Columbus, Ohio to interview the first $64,000 winner on *Question*, former Marine Capt. Richard McCutcheon. Since he lives out of state, McCutcheon hasn't been called before the New York grand jury; but he has sent a letter to the

Grand Jury Association of New York County confessing his "personal feelings of shame" about his win. McCutcheon tells Stone of being coached by Mert Koplin and how his family members urged him to continue because he did legitimately know the answers to the questions.

Stone wrote: "Despite his affluence, life did not go well for McCutcheon; he left the Marine Corps and separated from his wife in 1957. For all his intelligence, talent, good looks, and energy, it seemed that he had gained little or nothing from being a quiz star. A moralistic streak and a profound fear of being exposed had induced deep feelings of shame and anxiety in him."[3]

***

In Washington, a young attorney reads about Schweitzer's sealing of the grand jury's presentment in *The New York Times*.[4] Boston-born Richard Goodwin is fresh out of Harvard Law School and a newly-hired associate counsel at the U.S. House Subcommittee on Legislative Oversight. It is an adjunct of the House Committee on Interstate and Foreign Commerce, which has jurisdiction over all federal administrative agencies including, among many others, the Federal Communications Commission.

Goodwin approaches the committee's chief counsel, Robert Lishman, with the article.

"There must be something there," Goodwin says. "If there was nothing wrong, then why keep it a secret?" Lishman agrees, and on July 30, an investigation into quiz shows is announced by the Commerce committees in the U.S. House and in the Senate.[5]

House Commerce Committee chairman Rep. Oren Harris says in a press statement:

"The great attraction of television quiz shows was the spectacle of the unknown genius whose wizardry and intellect baffled the nation. The winners of these shows became folk heroes, and their daily activities were followed on the front pages of the nation's newspapers. These programs attracted immense viewing audiences, resulting in large profits to producers and sponsors. We now have information leading us to suspect that contestants on some of the shows were coached and given answers in order to enhance their audience appeal. If this is true, the American people have been deceived on a large scale."[6]

Goodwin goes to New York to begin his investigation. There he receives a warm welcome from ADA Joseph Stone. Goodwin later wrote:

"I was surprised. . . . there was no sign of resentment at my unmasked intrusion. Stone was that rarest of public servants, concerned with uncovering and disclosing the truth, wherever credit might go."[7]

Goodwin appears before Judge Schweitzer and asks for the grand jury minutes to be released to the subcommittee. Schweitzer grants the request.

Despite Goodwin's goodwill, Stone is not as onboard with the idea as it might seem. He is worried that names of those who testified might be released. He will later write:

"From the beginning, I had confidently assured former contestants that if they came clean, their testimony would be sacrosanct except in the event of a public trial of criminal charges."[8]

Goodwin counter-argues that the committee plans only to ask people to volunteer their testimony.

"This jerk Goodwin double-crossed me," Stone later tells writer Jeff Kisseloff. "[He] promised to use [the minutes] only for reference and perhaps to cross-examine witnesses. If the witness lied before the grand jury they could confront him only with _his_ grand jury testimony. But Goodwin was a wily opportunist."[9]

The rest of the summer is spent transcribing the voluminous grand jury minutes and rounding up witnesses for the House subcommittee hearings. Stone later wrote:

"I had occasional calls from the mercurial Goodwin, asking for addresses and phone numbers of former contestants and others. Goodwin was spending a great deal of time in New York but did not share his findings with me. When I heard no complaints of harassment, I hoped it meant that Goodwin was adhering to the tacit agreement not to turn the public spotlight on the former contestants who had cooperated with us. . . . Goodwin had assumed what amounted to carte blanche authority as a congressional investigator. [He] boasted how he had terrorized producers, advertising men, former contestants, and others by brandishing blank subpoenas signed by [Congressman] Harris."[10]

In his autobiography, *Remembering America*, Goodwin recounts meeting with both Herbert Stempel and Charles Van Doren during his investigation.

He and Van Doren meet one morning just after one of Van Doren's regular appearances on the *Today* show.

"Absolutely calm, with friendly but never overeager amiability, he answered my questions about the quiz shows. . . . He could not, of course, speak for other contestants, he told me, but his own appearance had been exactly what it seemed. . . . 'And look at the result. Not the money, although it certainly came in handy. . . . But I'm the only person who reads poetry on television. I'm a teacher, you know, and now I can reach millions. All because of the quiz shows.' "[11]

Goodwin continued, "I wanted to believe Van Doren. . . . He seemed to believe, must believe, what he was saying. . . . The depths of the human mind have hiding places for the most contradictory recollections and beliefs; desires whose powerful surge can overpower conscious knowledge and awareness."[12]

Both men come from Eastern. educated backgrounds and there is a bond between them. Yet at the same time, Goodwin and Van Doren begin playing a game of cat and mouse.

Goodwin shares with Van Doren his notes from an interview with indicted *Twenty-One* producer Albert Freedman, in which he admits to coaching Van Doren.

"I know you're lying, Charlie," Goodwin tells him. "We can prove it."

"I'm sorry you feel that way, Dick," he responds.

Goodwin also tells Van Doren that if he keeps quiet, he will not be subpoenaed by the congressional subcommittee.

"After the hearings begin," Goodwin says, "you must make no statements. Don't say anything. Go hide in the country if you have to. Because if you defend yourself publicly, you'll force the committee to call you."[13]

***

On Tuesday, October 6, 1959, the congressional quiz show hearings begin with witnesses connected with *Twenty-One* and *Dotto*.[14]

Chairman Harris opens the hearings in the house Caucus Room by stating that the testimony of *Twenty-One* producers Dan Enright and Albert Freedman, who was charged with perjury by the grand jury, will be in executive session.

"This was the first indication to me," Stone wrote, "that the quiz hearings would be a three-ring circus. In the center ring would be the performances of those testifying in the open. In a side ring, obscured from the public as it happened but revealed later . . . would be a series of closed sessions, stage-managed in great part by Enright. In the third ring, revealed only in glimpses at first, was the show that would most intrigue the public — the drama of the fate of Charles Van Doren."[15]

The lead-off witness is Herbert Stempel.

Before a congressional subcommittee, Herbert Stempel once again relates details about his rigged run on *Twenty-One*.

He tells the story that, by now, he has told many times about his involvement in the rigging on *Twenty-One* and his coaching by Dan Enright. He recalls how Enright told Stempel that he would have to lose "for the good of the show" and that Enright promised him perks and a possible new job "if I kept my mouth shut."[16]

Stempel then recalls his final appearance on the show — how he was instructed to throw a question about the film *Marty* and lose to Charles Van Doren. A kinescope of that show is shown to the panel.

Stempel is then questioned by members of the committee — some more seriously than others.

Congressman Walter Rogers of Texas: "They asked you to do a lot of things?"

Stempel: "That is correct, sir."

Rogers: "Did they ever make you drink any [*Twenty-One* sponsor] Geritol?"

Stempel:" Frankly speaking, I couldn't see spending $2.98 for 25 cents worth of cheap medicine."[17]

Other congressmen zero in on the as-yet unheard from Charles Van Doren.

Congressman Steven Derounian of New York: "Mr. Van Doren has built himself up as an intellectual giant in the eyes of the American people and is making a lot of money today on Dave Garroway's program [*Today*] telling sweet stories of art, poetry, and compassion for humankind. Is it reasonable to assume, based upon your information, that Mr. Van Doren also got the Enright preparation and treatment throughout these programs he participated in?"

Stempel: "May I say, sir — I believe you watched the kinescopes and watched the identical actions. I would assume that two gentlemen under pressure do not have the exact same patterns when they are nervous. Some people whom I know pull ears, scratch heads, sneeze, cough, et cetera. When two people bite lips, scratch heads, mop brows, and act identically alike, I would venture to say that the treatment was probably of the same."[18]

Next up is James Snodgrass, the *Twenty-One* contestant who mailed registered letters to himself containing answers that he was coached on. He connects Freedman to the coaching.[19]

Before the panel, Snodgrass opens one of the letters he sent himself and reads aloud:

"To whom it may concern: The following are some of the questions, specifically the ones I will be asked for the television quiz show *Twenty-One* on the night of May 13. First category: Movies. I take 11 points. The question is worth 11 points. 'In the story of *Snow White and the Seven Dwarfs*, after she is banished from the palace of her stepmother, the Queen, Snow White goes to live in the forest with seven dwarfs. In the Walt Disney version. what were the names of the seven dwarfs? (I shall answer in this sequence — Sleepy, Sneezy, Dopey, Happy (pause), the grouchy one, Grumpy (pause), Doc (pause), Bashful.")[20]

Snodgrass outlines how he became a contestant on *Twenty-One* — completing a test to determine his knowledge, taking part in a dress rehearsal and being interviewed by producer Albert Freedman.

"He told me that I would definitely be on the following Monday. I had looked good in the dress rehearsal which I imagined they watched through monitors. He suggested I have my teeth cleaned and to wear an off-white shirt, not a white shirt. It was at this time, I think, . . . where he told me what the questions and answers were to be for the first show."[21]

The next day, *The New York Times* reports, "The House subcommittee won access to the minutes and transactions of the grand jury's proceedings. It was obvious today that many of the questions asked . . . were based on the grand jury's work."[22]

***

The second day of testimony begins with two publicity agents who formerly worked with Barry & Enright Productions — Alfred Davis and Arthur Franklin. They testify that when news of Stempel's accusations broke, the network did virtually no investigation on its own.

Says Davis: "By [NBC's] reluctance at first to issue a strong statement backing Barry and Enright, they made it quite obvious that they wanted something more than mere indignation on our part. . . . Somebody on our team volunteered the information that there was evidence that Stempel was not a reliable witness."[23]

Davis and Franklin were then subpoenaed to appear before the grand jury, and beforehand they met with Dan Enright and an attorney named Edwin Slote. As they recount it, the session played like a perverse parody of how contestants were "prepped" on *Twenty-One*.

Chief Counsel Lishman: "Did [Slote] tell you to commit perjury before the grand jury?"

Davis: "He called it 'preparing the witness.' "

Lishman: "Did he tell you to deny matters which you knew were true?"

Davis: "Yes, sir."

And Davis, ever the PR pro, endeavors to spin his testimony as much as possible:

Lishman: "Did he tell you to do this while you were under oath?"

Davis: "I could not swear to that, sir."

Lishman; "Did you receive this advice from Mr. Slote to the effect that you were not to testify truthfully before the grand jury that you knew Stempel had received questions and answers and what the circumstances were which led you to believe that he had received the questions and answers?"

Davis: "I don't know if the grand jury came in, but in my mind at the time the district attorney's office and the grand jury were all lumped into one. . . . [Slote] did tell me what you say. I don't know whether he mentioned grand jury."[24]

Franklin, who was Davis's partner at the time, is also no slouch at spinning. When discussing a conference with NBC executives about Stempel's charges, Lishman asked Franklin how he approached it.

"There was a delicate balance that I always maintained," Franklin says. "I talked directly but in a vague way."[25]

But Franklin is considerably more direct about his feelings regarding Dan Enright and Jack Barry.

"I had known Jack Barry and Dan Enright for many years. They had always been very decent people up until this situation with the *Twenty-One* show. They always behaved in a very open and above[-]board manner. Dan Enright was one of the nicest people I ever met before he got greedy enough to enter into such an unholy alliance. Jack Barry was a lot simpler. I knew Jack very well. I would describe Jack as a kindergarten egomaniac. He suffers the same as most people do who like to appear on television and be recognized on the streets. Dan Enright was a different kind of man. I considered Dan as a superior person in those days. He was extremely well-educated and conversant with many things we liked to discuss. I thought it was a shame he had gone so far."[26]

Next up after Franklin is *Twenty-One* contestant Rose Leibbrand, whose one-episode appearance occurred as Herbert Stempel was beginning his ascent. Leibbrand testifies that before she appeared on the show, Albert Freedman ordered her to bid no higher than seven or eight points.

"I realized when I was in the booth when I was given [the same questions that were in the warmup] that the show was fixed," she says. "I realized it was rigged when I was absolutely prohibited, so to speak, from bidding more than seven or eight. I was a little cha-grined."[27]

Then comes another contestant. Richard Jackman, who testi-fies to being coached by Enright. Jackman defeated three oppo-nents and won $24,500, but felt it was improper and didn't want to continue. He says that, in exchange for appearing on several more shows, Enright offered him $100 a week for the rest of his life with the winnings he could amass. Jackman refused, and Enright gave him a check for only $15,000. Any more than that, he told Jackman, would throw the show's budget "out of whack."[28]

Jackman took the money, he says, because "I wanted to be as far out of the business as I could but I wanted to assuage some of my family's misfortune, I guess, or surprise and disappointment."[29] After his testimony, he admits to reporters that he later threatened to sue for, and received, the remaining $9,500 from Enright.[30]

The first representative of a sponsor then takes the stand. He is Edward Kletter, vice president and director of advertising at Phar-maceuticals, Inc., the makers of Geritol and the sponsor of *Twen-ty-One*. Straight out of the gate he denies any interference in the operations of the show.

Chief Counsel Lishman: "At any time in your conversation with Mr. Enright or representatives of Barry and Enright, did you discuss the contestants that Pharmaceuticals would like to have continued on the show, because of their pulling appeal to the public?"

Kletter:" Never."

Lishman: "Did you ever have conversations with Enright, let us say, at lunch, at which you would indicate to him, 'So-and-so is doing very well. I certainly hope he continues on the program'? "

Kletter: "Oh, yes. I, the same as 40 million other Americans."[31]

Lishman: "When did you first learn that in the show *Twenty-One*, assurance had been given to contestants by Barry and Enright?"

Kletter: "The day I read it in the *Journal-American*, I believe, the same as everyone else did."

Lishman: "About what was that date?"

Kletter:" I would say sometime in August of 1958. I was shocked, I might say."

Lishman: "Did anyone in your organization have any knowledge of this, do you believe?"

Kletter: "No, I do not believe so."

Lishman: "How closely did you follow these programs?"

Kletter:"In what way, sir?"

Lishman: "In determining the quality appeal they were having to the buying public?"

Kletter: "Frankly, I was an enthusiast of the show and *The $64,000 Question* and the other quiz shows, as many millions of other people were, and I watched them at home with as much enthusiasm, admiration, and awe as anyone else may have done. We personally did not in any way — that is, we the sponsor, or the agency — have anything whatever to do with the production of the program itself. Our only concern was with the production of our commercials on the program."[32]

When asked how and when the decision was made to cancel *Twenty-One*, Kletter says:

"I think after we got involved in it more and after we got all the stories and after we met with Mr. Stone and the grand jury, then we began to smell that probably something — I believe we were mad. We did not take this lying down. We finally decided that there is something behind this and we cancelled forthwith and we would have done it two years ago if we had found out that Mr. Stempel was being coached even after the third program. We would have forthwith cancelled without any question."[33]

After denying a press request that his photo be taken, Kletter steps down.

The next witness, NBC vice president and general attorney Thomas Ervin, reads a boilerplate statement about how seriously the network takes any quiz accusations, and then presents proof: He announces that the network has fired Howard Felsher, producer of NBC-owned *Tic Tac Dough*, for refusing to sign a sworn statement that no rigging ever took place on the show. He also testifies that NBC was "very badly deceived" by Enright regarding *Twenty-One*, while also admitting the network did very little to look into Stempel's allegations.[34]

That night, Dan Enright and Albert Freedman testify before the subcommittee in a closed-door executive session that lasts until 1 a.m.

The next day, NBC stops short of firing Charles Van Doren but relieves him of his network duties, including his regular spot on *Today*. On the air, *Today* host Dave Garroway emotionally praises Van Doren's honesty and character.[35]

Over the next few days, a parade of contestants, producers and behind-the-scenes staff all take the stand in Washington.

Another *Dotto* winner, Antoinette DuBarry Hillman, says she was indirectly coached, but she never broached the subject with the producers. "[W]e played the whole thing like a solemn minuet, like everybody bowing and smiling and taking you back and forth and pretending nothing at all was going on. We would have these little talks, but we never came clean with each other. We got very cozy. I was perfectly blithe about [the rigging]. They were having a happy time. I was, everyone was."[36]

A congressman asks Hillman if she thought there was any difference between a "battle of fists" in a sporting contest and a "battle of wits" on a quiz show.

"Well," she replies, "most boxers don't have sponsors."[37]

Eric Leiber, a *Dotto* artist, testifies that after every show, the producer had a "meeting . . . to decide what would happen on the next show."[38]

Kirsten Falke, a *Tic Tac Dough* contestant who was 16 at the time she was on the show, tells the subcommittee that now-fired producer Howard Felsher asked her to lie before the New York grand jury.[39]

Also testifying is Falke's mother, Irene Kitzing, who says, "if adults want to behave unethically, that is their business. They have their own conscience to live with. But when a youngster is asked to commit perjury or at least is being led along that direction, then I think it is disgraceful."[40]

Edward Hilgemeier, the original *Dotto* whistleblower, tells the subcommittee he is now unemployable in show business because of his actions. He also says he is suing *Tonight* host Jack Paar for libelous statements made about him on the air.[41]

Enright's closed-door testimony is made public. He has told the panel that the fixing of quiz shows has been "a practice for many, many years."[42]

"I think," he says, "being in an industry for 20 or 25 years, you would have to be very unsophisticated or very naive not to understand that certain controls have to be exercised. Now, the extent of the controls is something else."[43]

Freedman's testimony is similar:

"By the time I had taken over the production reins of *Twenty-One*, I had been in the entertainment field for approximately six years. . . . I have learned that a show, in order to be successful, had to be — for the most part needed control of sorts."[44]

"Control" is also alluded to by *Dotto* producer Ed Jurist:

"Every effort was made to control the shows. . . . Everything that happened on the show happened according to the desires of the producer. . . . Primary procedure was to find out what people knew and frame questions accordingly. The second procedure, to inculcate is a word I like to use, the people with information you thought they ought to have in such a way that they ideally were not aware you were doing it."[45]

On the question of morality, Jurist is sanguine:

"If [the contestants] were lucky they won a lot of money; if they were not so lucky they won a little money. They were not injured or maimed. All they had was a lot of fun. . . . I don't consider that immoral, particularly if you have grown up in the entertainment business as I have."[46]

But U.S. Representative John Moss of California is having none of it.

"I have two small daughters," he says. "They were very ardent fans of these programs. These youngsters now know that those were just as phony as they could be. . . . I say it is rotten, right down to the ground . . . you have created problems for every youngster who watched them and who had confidence in them. I think it is symptomatic of some far more basic problems in this whole industry with you people in a mad rush to develop something which is salable, which will draw a greater dollar, without any regard to a public obligation. I think it is one of the most demoralizing influences, as it is operated and as it is exposed, that we have present in this country today."[47]

Chairman Harris then reports that the subcommittee has received a telegram from Charles Van Doren, offering his testimony.[48]

Goodwin would later write, "I was stunned. He had been warned. He knew what evidence we had. The man must want to destroy himself."[49]

Stone would later tell an interviewer, "Van Doren was summoned to the office of some of the NBC executives . . . [t]hey pressured Van Doren to send a telegram [to the congressional subcommittee] volunteering to testify that he did not get the answers. To this day, that doesn't make any sense to me. All he had to say to NBC was, 'Gentlemen, I'm sorry. I have already testified before the grand jury and that's it.' . . . Instead, he sends them this telegram, which in effect dared them to call his bluff, and they took him up on it. They knew he was lying. . . . If Van Doren hadn't been such a schmuck and sent that telegram he would never have been subpoenaed. The worst thing that could have happened to him was NBC got rid of him. He would have made a terrific settlement with them because in his contract there was nothing that said he had to be morally correct."[50]

Chairman Harris accepts the offer and awaits Van Doren's response.

Next up is Sy Fischer of Frank Cooper Associates, the company that produced *Dotto* for Colgate-Palmolive. He echoes Jurist that the show was simply entertainment and that there was no shortage of people wanting to play the game.

"The only people we wanted to put on the *Dotto* program were people who wrote us and said they wanted to appear, and there were millions. We have received a million cards in a week. They then were treated, screened, handled by the production assistants in preparing them for the show. But they didn't have to cooperate."[51]

On the third day of hearings, October 9, the subcommittee hears first from advertising executive Richard A.R. Pinkham of the Ted Bates agency, representing Colgate-Palmolive on *Dotto*. When asked if *Dotto* was controlled, he demurs:

"I wouldn't say the word 'control' would be the one I would choose. I would think 'supervision' would be more to the point. Actually the agency's principal function is in the area of seeing to it that the commercials which they have produced for the client are properly placed and properly produced in the body of the show."[52]

Pinkham then dramatically recounts finding out about Hilgemeier's discovery of *Dotto* answers in Marie Winn's notebook.

Chief Counsel Lishman: "When did it come to your attention that Marie Winn, one of the contestants on *Dotto*, had been previously given the answers to questions to be asked her on the show?"

Pinkham: "My first acquaintance with this was a shocking meeting that occurred in my office at 9 o'clock on a Friday morning . . . when the vice-president in charge of advertising for the Colgate Company, my client, appeared at this unearthly hour in my office and said he had received a call from Mr. Hilgemeier. As I remember, we told them about this statement from Hilgemeier . . . to the best of my recollection they replied there was no truth in his statement but nonetheless they had paid him $1,500. I remembered reacting to this, this seemed like an idiotic thing to do, and to a certain extent an admission of some guilt."[53]

As an ad executive — one with two middle initials, yet — Pinkham is far above the fray of daily production, and can easily blame the whole affair on underlings:

"To be sure," he says, "one of the things we discovered when we started our investigation was the low level of security given to not only the cards [containing questions and answers] but also to the *Dotto* caricatures and to the clues. We found that there was a very poor security."[54]

Dan Enright's name comes up again in testimony by Howard Felsher, the producer of *Tic Tac Dough* who was let go because he refused to swear that contestants hadn't been given answers in advance.

Chief Counsel Lishman: "Is it a fact that up to the fall of 1958, 75 percent of these evening performances [of *Tic Tac Dough*] . . . were ones in which at least one of the contestants had been furnished the questions and answers in advance of the show itself?"

Felsher: "I would say it is in that vicinity."

Lishman: "Were you the person that furnished the questions and answers to such contestants?"

Felsher: "Yes, I was."

Lishman: "And Mr. Enright knew that you were doing this?"

Felsher: "Yes, he did."[55]

Felsher is also asked about Army Capt. Michael O'Rourke and his rigged run on *Tic Tac Dough*. At first, Felsher wraps himself in the flag:

Felsher: "I would like to point out, if I can, that Captain O'Rourke carries in his body over a dozen pieces of shrapnel that he acquired in Korea."

Chairman Harris: "What?"

Felsher: "Captain O'Rourke carries in his body over a dozen pieces of shrapnel that he acquired in Korea when he won the Distinguished Service Cross."

Harris: "As much as I sympathize with any injured veteran . . . it does not give anybody a license because of that very fact then to return and commit fraud or any other act on the American people."[56]

On Monday, October 12, the subcommittee adjourns temporarily. In the past six days there have been nationwide headlines about the testimony. The networks are busy covering their tracks and purging any remaining big-money quizzes from their schedules. And Charles Van Doren still hasn't been heard from. In fact, he can't be found.

CHAPTER SEVEN: "I WAS INVOLVED, DEEPLY INVOLVED, IN A DECEPTION" (OCTOBER 1959-JANUARY 1962)

"For a television quiz-show rigger, life in the late
Nineteen Fifties was no bed of roses."
— Russell Baker of The New York Times *on*
the congressional testimony of Mert Koplin,
producer of The $64,000 Question, *on November 3, 1959*[1]

Because there has been no further response from Charles Van Doren about testifying before the subcommittee, their invitation has been changed to a subpoena — one that subcommittee chairman Rep. Oren Harris accuses Van Doren of avoiding.

From October 9 to October 13, Charles Van Doren is missing.

His classes at Columbia University are cancelled.

His phone is disconnected.

"Where's Charlie?" is the headline in the New York *Journal-American* on October 13. And the next day he reappears in Manhattan for a hastily organized press conference.

"Mr. Van Doren said he went to New England the previous Thursday not to avoid the subpoena but 'to find solace' — he 'walked the woods and climbed mountains' with his wife. He noted that that day he had been 'distressed' by the NBC suspension . . . and by the efforts of newsmen to reach him, his family and his friends. . . . Mr. Van Doren said he did not know about the subpoena, which he observed had caused so 'much unfortunate misunderstanding.'"[2]

Arrangements are made for Van Doren to appear before the subcommittee on November 2. In the meantime, he resumes teaching at Columbia.

It's also reported that the subcommittee will begin looking into rigging on *The $64,000 Question* and *The $64,000 Challenge*. The original producer of *Question*, CBS Television President Lou Cowan, tells the press that he is "in a position to comment on the actual production of *The $64,000 Question* only for the seven-week period I was at the production company. During that period there was no rigging of the program so far as I know and if there had been, I think I would have known about it."[3]

On October 16, CBS Network President Frank Stanton makes a speech to the Radio and Television News Directors Association acknowledging the network's failure to "meet our duty" with regard to quiz shows. He says the network's intent is to be "masters in our own house" over "everything that appears on the CBS Television Network — and I mean everything."[4] The network announces the cancellation of the rest of its big-money quizzes — *Name That Tune*, *Top Dollar* and *The Big Payoff*. In fact, the network says it will ban all "deceits" — even advance looks at the questions being asked celebrities on *Person to Person* and the use of canned laughter.[5]

On October 22, President Dwight Eisenhower says at a press conference that "Fixing TV shows was a terrible thing to do to the public."[6]

And on November 1, *The New York Times* reports on what could be the first actual crime attached to the shows — that a department store owner, Max Hess, paid $10,000 to production personnel on *The $64,000 Question* to place a Hess employee as a contestant who would plug the store on the air.[7]

***

On Monday, November 2, 1959, Charles Van Doren walks into the Caucus Room. Among the spectators are his father, author and professor Mark Van Doren; his wife, Geraldine; and Herbert Stempel.

ADA Stone writes: "Without preliminaries Harris swore in Van Doren, who began with a well-crafted, prepared statement, which took him some ten minutes to read, without the gestures of hesitation and mental strain that had made him famous. The only signs of nervousness where a jiggling foot and almost constant smoking."[8]

Van Doren: "I would give almost anything I have to reverse the course of my life in the last three years. I've learned about life. I've learned about myself, and about the responsibilities any man has to his fellow men. I've learned a lot about good and evil. They are not always what they appear to be. I was involved, deeply involved, in a deception. The fact that I, too, was very much deceived cannot keep me from being the principal victim of that deception, because I was its principal symbol. There may be a kind of justice in that. I don't know. . . . I have deceived my friends, and I had millions of them. Whatever their feeling for me now, my affection for them is stronger today than ever before."[9]

He continues, "I had supposed I would win a few thousand dollars and be known to a small television audience. But from an unknown college instructor, I became a national celebrity. I received thousands of letters and dozens of requests to make speeches, appear in movies, and so forth. To a certain extent, this went to my head. I was winning more money than I ever dreamed of having. I was able to convince myself that I could make up for it after it was over. . . . I didn't know what to do or where to turn, and frankly, I was very much afraid."[10]

He says that Stempel's allegations left him "horror-struck." "I was at the time appearing on the Garroway program [*Today*] as a replacement for Mr. Garroway, who was on vacation. I have said I received many letters. Thousands more were from schoolchildren and students. All expressed their faith in me . . . and so I made a statement on the Garroway program the next morning to the effect that I knew of no improper activities on *Twenty-One* . . . I knew that most people would believe me. Most people did."

Of his recent disappearance, Van Doren says, "I simply ran away
. . . Most of all, I was running from myself. . . . My life and career
were being swept away in a flood. I tried to save whatever part
seemed in the most immediate danger."[11]

It wasn't until he returned to New York, Van Doren says, that it
became clear what he had to do. It happened when he read a letter
from a stranger.

"She told me that the only way I could ever live with myself,
and make up for what I had done — of course, she, too, did not
know exactly what it was — was to admit it, clearly, openly, truly.
Suddenly, I knew she was right. And this way, which had seemed
so long the worst possible of all alternatives, suddenly became
the only one. Whatever the personal consequences, and I knew
they would be severe, this was the only way. In the morning I tele-
phoned my attorney and told him my decision. . . . He said, 'God
bless you.'"[12]

In Washington, *Twenty-One* contestant Charles Van Doren is again
before the cameras following his public confession to a congressional
subcommittee on November 2, 1959.

Most of the congressmen fall over themselves congratulating
Van Doren for his candor and only gently chide him for his part in
the deception.

Walter Rogers of Texas: "[T]he American people are against corruption but they are for forgiveness when a man comes in and tells the truth. . . . It took a long time to get you to do it, but when you did, I don't think you left any stones unturned."[13]

Says Chairman Oren Harris: "[A]nyone, regardless of how it hurts, who comes to tell the whole truth in a matter so important to the American people and the public interest is to be highly complimented. . . . I could end this session with you by saying what your attorney did say to you the other day; that is, 'God bless you.'"[14]

Steven Derounian of New York is a little saltier: "I don't think an adult of your intelligence should be commended for telling the truth."[15]

That afternoon Van Doren's resignation is accepted by Columbia University and his career at NBC is hanging by a thread. But for the most part, the press is sympathetic.

"For the moment," editorializes the *New York Post*, "our question is this: how many men identified with the big and little fixes of life, with the spurious commercial, the fake promotion and all the other articles of financial gamesmanship, are resuming business as usual this morning now that Charles Van Doren has walked into his lonely exile?"[16]

Says columnist Fulton Lewis Jr.: "The self-destruction of Charles Van Doren took place prior to the congressional hearing, when he appeared under oath before the New York Grand Jury and knowingly lied to try to save himself; when he sent the Committee a knowingly false telegram for the same reason; when he held up and holed up for days, until the evidence against him had so massed itself that there was no hope of saving himself with further lies. . . . It is always tragic to see a man destroy himself, for whatever reason. When the reason is money and the man is young and promising, it is the more so."[17]

Says columnist Dorothy Kilgallen: "Now that his whole story has been told, I feel he is being flayed without mercy by people who find comfort in the sins of others — especially the sins of those who are famous and have been held in high esteem. . . . Van Doren did wrong, there is no question about it. But he is not a murderer or a rapist or a kidnapper. I would like to see Georgetown University, or Notre Dame, or Villanova offer him a teaching post as a demonstration that true contrition is as acceptable to man as well as to God."[18]

Just before Van Doren's testimony, *Broadcasting* magazine commissions a national survey about quiz shows. More than half of the respondents want to see the shows back on the air and only a few say the congressional investigation has affected their attitude toward TV.[19]

The same survey is conducted a day after Van Doren's testimony, and television takes a hit. Now over 50% say their attitude toward TV has been affected, and fewer viewers want to see quizzes back on the air. Almost 50% agree with Columbia University's decision to fire Van Doren, but they also believe that producers are most to blame.[20]

Public comment, as registered by the surveys, conveys that most people come down on one of two sides: 1) "This is a violation of trust. These shows were presumed to be honest — the newspapers covered them like legitimate sporting events." 2) "We knew it all along! Who cares, anyway? It's just a TV show!"

His testimony complete, Van Doren tells a reporter, "I feel better than I have for three years." He and his wife leave the Caucus Room.[21]

The next day Van Doren writes a letter to Richard Goodwin, to whom he has grown close over the course of the investigation.

"Hunters," he writes, "used to say that the stag loved the hunter who killed it . . . thus the tears, which were the tears of gratitude and affection. Something like that *does* happen, I know. And Raskolnikov [protagonist of *Crime and Punishment*] felt the same. Thus Gerry and I do extend an invitation to you to come and I wish you would come. There are a number of things I'd like to talk to you about — none of them having to do with quiz shows. I made the mistake of reading the papers. I should have taken your advice. I wish the next six months were already over. . . . But I am trying to tell you that we will live and thrive, I think — I mean I know we will live and I think we will thrive — and that you must never, in any way, feel any regret for your part in this."[22]

In the days before widespread shamelessness, in the days before celebrity redemption arcs, in the days before bad behavior is milked for more air time, Charles Van Doren has the fortitude, the self-respect — the decency? — to simply do the one thing that the disgraced never seem to do in today's society.

He disappears.

***

Van Doren's exit from the Caucus Room is almost immediately followed by the entrance of Stoney Jackson, who tells the panel the *$64,000 Challenge* stories recounted in Chapter Four.

"I have not been censured nearly so much for taking the money as for opening my big mouth," he tells the congressmen.[23] "The fact that I am an ordained minister does not make me a saint."[24]

He adds: "Most of us have a good bit of larceny in us, if we admit it, because this is an age where a lot of respect is directed toward a man with money and a good deal of looking askance at the man who doesn't have it, regardless of what the consequences might be."[25]

Next up is Arthur Cohn, who recounts his story of losing on *The $64,000 Challenge* and learning that his opponent, Wilton Springer, was fed questions in advance. Both name associate producer Shirley Bernstein as the woman who did the coaching.

"[Cohn] said that when Mr. Springer was asked the same questions on the air, 'I felt like I was going to blurt the entire thing out . . . it was just cheating.' He said he remained silent because 'no one wants a troublemaker.' " He says that he contacted Bernstein after the show and she spoke of an "amazing coincidence."[26]

The next day, the subcommittee hears from two more *$64,000 Challenge* contestants — bandleader Xavier Cugat and Patty Duke, now a budding young star thanks to her performance in the new Broadway play *The Miracle Worker*. Duke also connects Bernstein to being given answers. Cugat expresses regret that what he thought of as a publicity stunt became a kind of morality play.

"I thought it was entertainment — it was a show," he says. "If there was too much make believe, I wish you could do something about it without giving entertainment a black name."[27]

The man who coached Cugat, producer Mert Koplin, is next up. His initial contention is that, even if *The $64,000 Question* was controlled, the contestants never consciously knew of the control.

But there was control, he adds. The sponsor demanded it.

Reports *Broadcasting* magazine: "Mr. Koplin stated [that] when the 'controls' did not work in achieving the results on the show which Revlon officials wanted, the 'atmosphere' at the next weekly meeting was 'one of extreme displeasure . . . which took many forms.' . . . He said Revlon never threatened to 'get anyone's job' but that Martin Revson was 'unpleasant quite a good deal of the time.' The control actually was exercised by the sponsor, he said, and the producers were ordered to have more losers."[28]

Koplin's superior, executive producer Steve Carlin, agrees. After publicly proclaiming in *TV Guide* that *The $64,000 Question* was on the up and up, he has changed his tune.

"There is a tradition in television," he tells the panel, "of trying to please the client. If you have a client whom you see once in 13 weeks, pleasing becomes a relatively simple matter. But if you have a client whom you see each week, a very persuasive client, pleasing him becomes more difficult. You have to please him every week, not every 13 weeks. We were willing to please the client."[29]

Corroborating their testimony are memos from ad agency Batten, Barton, Durstine & Osborn outlining Revlon's control, and also a statement from one-time Revlon VP and Advertising Director George Abrams, who "said Revlon regularly suggested that especially tough questions be asked unpopular contestants to get them off show and that favorable contestants get easy ones."[30]

***

Later that day, a decision is made at NBC — the suspended Van Doren is now an ex-employee.

The network states, "Mr. Van Doren's admissions in his testimony are completely at variance with his repeated denials of complicity in or knowledge of any rigging on *Twenty-One* — denials made to the press, the New York County District Attorney, to the grand jury, to the viewing public, and his employers at NBC."[31]

The next morning, on the *Today* show, host Dave Garroway eulogizes his former colleague:

"[I am] still a friend of Charles Van Doren. . . . I can only say I am heartbroken. He was one of our family. We are a little family on this show, strange as it may seem. . . . Whatever Charles did was wrong, of course. I cannot condone or defend it. But we will never forget the non-Euclidean geometry essays or the poetry of Sir John Suckley which Charles left us with."[32]

On November 4, the subcommittee hears from the two men almost universally described as the ones behind the fixes on the *$64,000* shows — the Revson brothers, Charles and Martin.

Charles Revson, the mercurial head of Revlon, told congressional
investigators he was "flabbergasted" when he learned of the rigging
on *The $64,000 Question*. Wrote *Time* magazine: "[T]he thought of Charlie
Revson being flabbergasted was almost more than the cosmetics industry
could bear. When it comes to business, Revson not only knows all the
answers, he knows the questions too."

First up is Martin. In a power struggle with his brother, he
has been ousted from the company (see Chapter Four), but like
the stockholder he remains, he is a steadfast defender of Revlon's
honor. When his statements are challenged by a congressman, he
snaps back, "You have no right to say I am not telling the truth."[33]
He paints Revlon as powerless to counteract the producer's plans.
"[They] had the last word on everything. If we didn't like it, there
was nothing we could do about it. [They] made it clear that they did
not need Revlon. They told us constantly that we were lucky to have
the show — that other sponsors were lined up at their door."[34]

Then comes Charles Revson.

Reports *Time*: "As sponsor of the rigged *$64,000 Question* and
$64,000 Challenge — which in four years helped triple Revlon's sales
to $111 million and boost its profits sevenfold to $9.7 million —
Revson was the center of a controversy over what part, if any, he
played in the rigging. Revson denied all, told a congressional committee: 'I was flabbergasted.' Wherever the truth lay, the thought of

Charlie Revson being flabbergasted was almost more than Madison Avenue and the cosmetics industry could bear. When it comes to business, Revson not only knows all the answers, he knows the questions too. . . . Revson is as calm as the eye of a hurricane about the controversy that whirls around him."[35]

Revson tells the panel he didn't hear any reports about possible rigging until last year, and echoes his brother that Revlon was the victim of the shows' producers.

"In view of the circumstances," he says, "we went along for the several years in sponsoring the show. We did not realize what it was. . . . I don't know how to answer it. It is part of a business experience."[36]

At a press conference the next say, President Eisenhower compares the scandals to the fixing of the 1919 series that involved the Chicago Black Sox. "I think I share the American general reaction of almost bewilderment that people could conspire to confuse and deceive the American people," he says. "Selfishness and greed occasionally get the ascendancy over those things that we like to think of as the ennobling virtues of man, his capacity for self-sacrifice, his readiness to help others."[37] He also promises that a Justice Department probe of quiz practices will be completed by the end of the year.

From behind-the-scenes control and rigging, the panel momentarily turns to the issue of outright kickbacks. The congressmen hear from Max Hess, the Allentown, Pennsylvania department-store owner, about paying $10,000 to get one of his employees onto *The $64,000 Question* as a contestant.[38] There are also reports that two audience warmer-uppers on the NBC quiz *Treasure Hunt* received payments in exchange for recommending particular contestants,[39] and that the Diebold safe company paid $30,000 over a three-year period to have a prop safe, prominently reading "Protected by Diebold, Inc.", featured on *The $64,000 Question.*[40]

The final two witnesses before the subcommittee are Frank Stanton, president of CBS, Inc., and Robert Kintner, president of

NBC. Both say they were unaware of any quiz rigging until last year. Neither one has any knowledge of the 1957 *Time* magazine article that first brought the idea of quiz controls to a wide audience.

The congressmen are skeptical.

John Bennett of Michigan: "I am sure that with the efficient organization that NBC has, somebody in the top echelon knew about the [*Time*] story. To let those stories go by the board . . . just seems to me not to be the right way to get to the facts."[41]

Stanton's excuse is that he was out of the country at the time.

"It may have been discussed, I don't know," he says. "I think you have to realize that these are competitors who are throwing the stones. The management of the publication that ran the article is the licensee of four affiliates of the networks that were carrying those programs. The same management that was privy to the information in that article continued to carry the programs that were being fed to them."[42]

Kintner says that NBC was able to handle the quiz problem by internal means, including through a kind of investigative corps made up of ex-FBI agents.

Stanton points to the new protections against "deceits" recently implemented by CBS, and adds this enigmatic statement: "I think the word 'control' is a dirty word when read against one situation and . . . a good or clean word when read against another. . . . Control isn't bad, but control with abuse is bad."[43]

On November 6, the hearings come to a close. The networks have promised to end the practice of coaching contestants in any way, but it's a moot point. The age of the sponsor-dominated program is beginning to die out, as advertisers with a product to sell begin spreading their commercial messages across different programs by buying individual spots on the schedule instead of entire blocks of time.

"The network[s]," says broadcast historian Erik Barnouw, "had been wanting for some time to get control over their own schedule.

. . . The networks used the scandals as an excuse to take over their own programming."[44]

The quiz show has morphed into the game show, exemplified by Goodson-Todman's *The Price Is Right* and Barry & Enright's *Concentration* — one where everyday people play uncomplicated games to win prizes rather than cash.

Meanwhile, the critics are heard from.

John Crosby: "The moral squalor of the quiz show mess reaches through the whole industry. Nothing is what it seems in television . . . the feeling of high purpose, of manifest destiny that lit the industry when it was young . . . is long gone."[45]

Adds Ralph McGill in the Washington *Evening Star*: "The quizzes revealed our deep, psychological lust for material 'things,' and greatly stirred up the wish, if not for easy money, then for an isolated booth in which to find it. I keep remembering a conversation with Carl Sandburg. 'Time,' he said, 'is the coin of your life. It is the only coin you have and only you can determine how it will be spent. Be careful lest you let other people spend it for you.' Those who faked the quiz shows spent a lot of it for a great many million Americans."[46]

The New York Times editorializes that the scandals focused attention "on a shocking state of rottenness within the radio-television world and on the 'get-rich-quick' schemes through which so many people were corrupted and so many millions deceived. What has been revealed is deplorable in respect to the level of public morality both in the industry and the individual."[47]

Mike Wallace, future *60 Minutes* co-anchor and one-time host of the quiz *The Big Surprise*, adds: "The networks must have the guts to stand up and say to the sponsor, 'I'll run my network; you sell your products. If you want to use us, O.K., but not on your terms.' "[48]

Ordinary viewers are also heard from.

Letters to *TV Guide*:

"... I simply hope Mr. Van Doren can learn of one unimportant American who is praying for his welfare." — T.G., Portsmouth, NH

"Anyone who thought they were on the up and up deserved to be fooled. I am delighted to say, 'I told you so.' " — H.B., Danville, PA

"If this is a sampling of the national conscience, then God help us all!" — Mrs. K.S., Florence, AZ

"Worms spoil apples. Mom spoiled me: And egghead Charlie spoiled TV." — G.B., Bonners Ferry, ID

"They smiled when Revson took the stand and claimed he did not know. But Revlon was the winner as the sales reports will show." — *H.F.W., Bradford, PA*[49]

Former *$64,000 Question* host Hal March is indignant as the hearings conclude and he threatens to sue Revlon.

"I feel deluded and used," March tells the press.[50] "The worst thing that happened on our program is that people won some money. If there was any monkey business on *The $64,000 Question,* I didn't know about it. It must have been on the level. We had some wonderful contestants who lost too soon. And we had a few people we would have liked to have dropped out of sight, but they kept winning."[51]

Thomas Kane (see Chapter Four), who won $100,000 on *Question* and *Challenge*, offers $1,000 to anyone who can prove the quizzes are rigged. "It is high time," he says, "that the producers who were in on the fixes came out with a list of genuine winners."[52]

Other former winners also come forward to deny any rigging.

"The show was on the level when I was on it," opera expert Gino Prato tells the Associated Press. "The sweat I put out from that [isolation] booth was true. I am in the clear. What I say to you, I say to God."

Adds baseball expert Myrt Power: "If somebody had been giving out answers I wouldn't have stopped at $32,000. I'd have gone all the way."

Shakespeare expert Redmond O'Hanlon says he received no overt help — but he also acknowledges that the questions may have been shaped for his strengths.[53]

On November 19, General Sessions Judge Mitchell Schweitzer finally rules on whether the grand jury's presentment of the previous June can be released. He says no. Newspapers criticize the decision and there are allusions to the old metaphor about closing the barn door after the horse has already escaped.[54]

"In the quiz matter," ADA Stone would later write, "Schweitzer danced to [Dan] Enright's tune."[55]

On December 8, although there is no evidence tying him to the fixing of *The $64,000 Question*, CBS forces the resignation of Louis Cowan as president of CBS-TV.[56]

At the end of the year. as Eisenhower promised, a "Report to the Public on Deceptive Practices in Broadcast Media" is released. The report leads to making it a federal crime to give or receive assistance on quiz shows.[57]

In June 1960, Assistant District Attorney Joseph Stone opens a second grand jury that re-interviews former contestants who have now admitted to lying to the grand jury. He is also investigating the alleged kickbacks to *The $64,000 Question* by department store owner Max Hess and the accusations of extortion against the two audience warmer-uppers on *Treasure Hunt*.

Finally, on January 27, 1962, Charles Van Doren, Elfrida Von Nardroff and Hank Bloomgarden — along with six other contestants who lied under oath — plead guilty to perjury.

Writes Stone: "Judge Breslin . . . was mellow when he asked for my recommendations in sentencing. I told the judge I had lived with the cases for a long time and was in a position to say how contrite the defendants were. No one involved could see any point in punishing them more than they already had been. Breslin suspended the sentences without imposing probation."[58]

CHAPTER EIGHT: AFTERMATH

"Charlie doesn't come out very much."
— a neighbor of Charles Van Doren, quoted in the
Redbook *magazine article "Aftermath of a Scandal"*[1]

As the dust settles from the quiz scandals, but before he has pled guilty to perjury, Charles Van Doren, his wife and their daughter are living on Bleecker Street in Greenwich Village. To make a living he is writing articles and books — all reportedly under a pseudonym.

When a writer with *Redbook* magazine asks for an interview, Van Doren declines.

"I think you can get a better picture of me without my telling you who I am," he says. "I can't stop you from talking to my friends. And anyway, my friends are better sources than I am. Don't your close friends know you better than you do yourself?"

One friend tells the writer, "Now he can be charming — a real cocktail-party conversationalist — when he wants to be. But he can also get into an intellectual argument and rip the other person to shreds, showing him no mercy. He doesn't let people off the hook. I don't mean to say he's become vicious — he's nice. He's affable, but he's very wry nowadays."[2]

Within a few years the Van Dorens will have relocated to Chicago. Longtime family friend Mortimer Adler has offered Van Doren a job with the *Encyclopedia Britannica* — soon he becomes an editorial director and will also write several more books, under his own name.

***

In 1968, hindsight is also offered by former CBS News president Fred W. Friendly. In his memoir, *Due to Circumstances Beyond Our Control,* he writes that he and long-time collaborator Edward R. Murrow almost became involved in their own quiz probe.

"In 1958, [CBS Director of Advertising] Bill Golden told Ed and me that there was some reason to believe that the big-money quiz shows were rigged, and that there was some damaging evidence. Bill wanted to know if we would be interested in doing a special documentary exposing the whole nasty mess; at least the company and the industry would then be exposing its own wrongdoings and this might considerably lessen the public's shock and revulsion. . . . We said that we would be interested in making such a report but that it would have to be done in our own way and on our terms, and that though we would welcome information from CBS, we would do our own investigating.

"But we never heard another word from Golden until long after the wreckage of the quiz shows had stunned everyone. 'Too bad you never did that *See It Now* on the quiz shows,' he said to me one day. When I asked him why he never mentioned it again, Bill told me that the lawyers had stopped it: 'They said it would have been in bad taste.' He added, 'Now what in hell do lawyers have to do with deciding what's good taste on the air and what isn't?'

"This conversation took place at lunch one day in October 1959. Bill kept talking about the shame of the quiz scandals and the congressional investigations, and what had happened to the company whose good name he had helped to create through all its formative years. Like Murrow, he was one of broadcasting's last angry men, and like Ed, he loved CBS. . . . As the lunch dishes were removed and the busboys set the tables for dinner, Bill's anger turned to sad despair about where the industry and CBS were headed. The last thing he said to me that afternoon was: 'You guys should have done that show.' Later his wife told me that he had talked about it all the way home that night. The next morning when I got to the cutting room, there was a message that Bill Golden had died in his sleep."[3]

***

By the early 1970s, after a brief exile in Florida, where they owned a radio station, the careers of Jack Barry and Dan Enright begin to bloom again. In 1972, the game show *The Joker's Wild* premieres on CBS, with Enright as producer and Barry as emcee. The show airs for three years on CBS and almost a decade in syndication, also hosted by Bill Cullen. It is revived, with Snoop Dogg as the emcee, in 2017.

***

In 1981, author Philip Roth memorializes Herbert Stempel in his novel, *Zuckerman Unbound,* as quiz contestant Alvin Pepler, still bitter over his loss to rival contestant Hewlitt Lincoln: "It was Alvin Pepler they cut down to make way for the great Hewlitt Lincoln. That is the subject of my book. The fraud perpetrated on the American public. The manipulation of the trust of tens of thousands of people. And how for admitting it I have been turned into a pariah until this day.

"The others involved have all gone on, onward and upward in corporate America, and nobody gives a good goddamn what thieves and liars they were . . . Alvin Pepler, to this day, is a dirty name throughout the American broadcasting industry . . . . All I wanted was for them to give me the subject, to let me study and memorize, and then to fight it out fair and square."[4]

***

In 1985, Charles Van Doren makes a brief appearance on the one TV show where he once was able to be himself — NBC's *Today.*

He is on to promote his book, *The Joy of Reading*, but he is also asked about his quiz experience.

He says: "That episode completely changed my life, and made me that man I am today. . . . I stopped teaching and became a reader, and a writer, and an editor. The last 20 years, last 25 years, have been truly wonderful, truly magical for me. Not just because I got into all that difficulty, but because I started consciously to create my life all over again. And I think that's probably a very good thing for people to do — to make their lives from scratch. I had to do it. But the result was something terrific for me. I went out to Chicago — I had 20 glorious years in Chicago. I worked for the *Encyclopedia Britannica* — those were great years. I was head of the editorial department. . . . Everything good that has happened to me resulted from what happened to me 25 years ago."

He stops and smiles.

"I only regret not being on the *Today* show, because I liked that so much."[5]

***

In his book *The Fifties*, David Halberstam writes:

"In the late 1980s, a distinguished television documentary maker named Julian Krainin was looking for a narrator-editor for a thirteen-part public television series on the history of philosophy. Krainin had read Van Doren's work, had loved *The Joy of Reading*, and was impressed by the powerful sweep of his intellect. Krainin, some fifteen years younger than Van Doren, had only the vaguest memory of the quiz-show scandals some thirty years after they had taken place. He contacted Van Doren, and gradually they began to agree on the outline of a public television series. They seemed to like each other and liked dealing with each other. Then Krainin's project hit a wall. The top people at PBS were wary about dealing with Van Doren until he himself dealt publicly with the quiz-show issue.

At that point Krainin suggested doing a documentary on the quiz-show scandals. It would clear the air, lance the boil, and prepare the way for the multipart show on philosophy. Krainin also pointed out that Van Doren himself, on a number of occasions when the subject came up, always said that he had nothing to hide and nothing to apologize for.

"Van Doren and Krainin went back and forth about doing a quiz-show documentary matter a number of times until one day Van Doren suddenly announced, 'I'm going to do it. I should have done this a long time ago.' But a few days later he called to say that he'd reconsidered. Krainin went ahead with his documentary, which was exceptionally well received and much praised for its fairness and sensitivity. Of the important players still living, only Charles Van Doren refused to participate."[6]

***

In 1988, Richard Goodwin, counsel in the Congressional quiz show investigations, publishes an autobiography, *Remembering America: A Voice from the Sixties.* It includes his experiences with the quiz scandals and his relationship with Van Doren. In 1992, Joseph Stone writes his own memoir, *Prime Time and Misdemeanors*, dense with information about the legal maneuvering in the case.

Krainin's documentary airs on the PBS series *American Experience* in early 1992. It includes interviews with Herbert Stempel, Dan Enright, Joseph Cates, Mert Koplin, Stoney Jackson and James Snodgrass.

The documentary is critically acclaimed, and in connection with Goodwin's book, the project attracts some attention in Hollywood.

***

In the fall of 1994, the story of Van Doren, Goodwin, Stempel and the *Twenty-One* rigging comes to the screen in *Quiz Show*. The film is directed by Robert Redford. Krainin is a co-producer. Paul Attansio's script follows the storyline in Goodwin's book. Herbert Stempel is a paid consultant.

Van Doren agrees to be involved at first, but bows out, and refuses to meet with Ralph Fiennes, who will play him in the film. Fiennes later tells *People* magazine that he appeared at Van Doren's door pretending to be lost so he could observe his movements and speech patterns. He says Van Doren seemed "sad."[7]

Despite the story's setting in the late 1950s, Redford told an interviewer he found it startlingly relevant.

"It has so much to do of where we are today . . . we can be numb, so cynical, and so shoulder-shrugging about major moral violations on our lives. It leaves us with this kind of eroded trust . . . primarily I saw it because it was a great story. But behind that, it was the beginning of a lot of things in our lives. a beginning of a loss of that trust. At that time everything we saw on television we believed was true . . . television was new and the merchants were trying to figure out how to get their hands on it, to control it, to manipulate this thing called mass audience. The country had this kind of wonderful innocent energy to it."[8]

Aside from Fiennes, the *Quiz Show* cast includes John Turturro as Herbert Stempel. Rob Morrow, fresh from the success of the TV series *Northern Exposure*, is Goodwin. David Paymer is Dan Enright, Christopher McDonald is Jack Barry and Paul Scofield plays Mark Van Doren. Hank Azaria plays Albert Freedman. Director Barry Levinson (*Rain Man*) plays *Today* host Dave Garroway and Martin Scorsese makes a cameo as Geritol CEO Matty Rosenhouse.

The film gets rave reviews.

Writes Joanne Kaufman in *People* magazine: "Without being schematic, [director Robert] Redford wisely focuses the story on the relationship between Fiennes, as a Connecticut WASP who sells his soul, and Morrow, as a Jewish kid from Brookline, Mass., who makes a clear choice to forswear material goods in favor of ethics. . . . *Quiz Show* goes on too long, and it can't resist a few sententious pronouncements about television. But these are small quibbles about a movie that solidly hits the jackpot."[9]

Duane Byrge in *The Hollywood Reporter*: "In this brilliant depiction of the early years of TV and the phenomenal powers it asserted in breaking down the walls of America's living rooms and homogenizing our culture, director Robert Redford has crafted a superb piece of cracked Americana."[10]

The film's release triggers a wave of "Where are they now?" stories as Van Doren keeps his silence.

"Please understand," he tells a reporter, "that I have a right to my privacy. Don't worry, we're friends, but please, I just don't want to talk about it."[11]

"I'm sure Charley hates all this being dredged up again," a Cornwall, Connecticut resident tells the Associated Press. "His father took it real hard. The old man was never the same after that."[12]

Goodwin tells *People* that Morrow spent several days with him, "absorbing my character. ... [H]e overdid my Boston accent."

About the hearings, he adds: "I think we accomplished something, but we were also disappointed" because the producers and sponsors escaped without blame. "I feel somewhat bad about the movie, for [Van Doren] having to be put through all of this again. . . . He told me [during the investigation] that it was like being in the bullring, with all of your family and friends around you, everybody cheering. There was no escape."[13]

If Van Doren shies from the spotlight when *Quiz Show* is released, Herbert Stempel devours it. He appears on *Entertainment Tonight* and on *Late Night with Conan O'Brien*, which is taped in the same studio, 6A, that once was the home of *Twenty-One*. To the audiences' delight, Stempel demands a rematch with Van Doren.[14]

"We've come full circle!" he says. "This time it's personal!"

Stempel is not as happy with Turturro's portrayal of him.

"I was a little miffed," he told an interviewer. "I was shown to be a nerd, a square and a hyper little guy." At the screening, he said, "John walked over to me and he said to me, 'If you punch me in the nose I would understand why.' . . . And I didn't want any trouble. I realized he played me over the top and so forth. He's an actor. He's told by the director, Redford, to play me in a certain way, and that's how he played it. And I said, 'No, John, everything's cool.'

"And my wife, Ethel, is a very feisty woman, and she said, 'Step aside, Herb, I want to take a crack at him.' "[15]

There's also some mild concern that, as the product at the center of the *Twenty-One* fix, there might be a backlash against Geritol, now being marketed as a vitamin supplement for women.

"It's a heavy knock," a marketing consultant tells *The New York Times*. "This is not something you'd pay to get into."[16]

Another consultant isn't concerned.

"Most moviegoers will regard it as history," says Clive Chajet, "and teenage moviegoers will regard it as ancient history."

He adds: "Charles Van Doren was my instructor at Columbia. He was dripping with class and intellectual integrity."[17]

Though *Twenty-One* producer Dan Enright has passed away, his son Don takes up his defense when the film is released.

He tells *The Hollywood Reporter*: "One of the things Dan really felt most troubled by, as he reflected on this time, was what he had done with Herb Stempel. That he had taken this man out of obscurity. That he had raised him on a great pedestal. And then he had brought him down and expected him to go away. And that he wasn't mindful or sensitive to Herb Stempel's sensitivities and to Herb Stempel's own humanity and what this would do to him. And clearly he paid an enormous price for that lack of sensitivity."[18]

***

In the summer of 1999, forty-four years after the premiere of *The $64,000 Question*, another big-money quiz show unites America around the tube.

Hosted by Regis Philbin, *Who Wants to Be a Millionaire?* features a similar format, with contestants answering steadily more difficult questions as they add to their winnings. There's also a "lifeline" added where contestants can ask for help from the studio audience or by phoning a friend.

Each episode is more self-contained, so there are no contestants' stories stretched over weeks. There's no dominant sponsor to control the show, and no need for overt rigging. At the end of the 1999-2000 season, *Who Wants to Be a Millionaire?* is airing three nights a week, and is in the top three Nielsen spots. Its appearance comes just before the rise of streaming and segmentation, making it close to the last gasp of water-cooler TV.[19]

***

In 2008, Charles Van Doren finally breaks his silence in the pages of *The New Yorker*, in an article titled "All the Answers." He recounts his time on *Twenty-One* and his coaching by Albert Freedman.

He also tells of being approached by the producers of *Quiz Show* to be a consultant — for $100,000.

The Van Dorens sit down with their two grown children for a family conference about what to do about the offer. His wife Geraldine prevails: "[T]aking the money gives them a kind of license. . . . I don't want anything to do with the whole thing. . . . Please don't be a fool."[20]

Van Doren agrees and declines the money. About the finished film, he writes:

"I understand that movies need to compress and conflate, but what bothered me the most was the epilogue stating that I never taught again. I didn't stop teaching, but it was a long time before I taught again in a college. I did enjoy John Turturro's version of Stempel. And I couldn't help but laugh when Stempel referred to me in the film as 'Charles Van Fucking Moron.' "[21]

More than anything else, however, the article recounts Van Doren's mental anguish and torture over his involvement in the rigging.

At one point in the article, Van Doren recounts a conversation with his father after leaving the show:

" 'I've never asked you about this whole experience, Charlie,' Dad said. . . . 'But I get the impression you're not too comfortable with your new fame — I mean, the way the quiz show may have changed your life. You may have many opportunities now that you might never have had before. But I've wondered if they're good — for you, being the man you are, or the man I think you are.'

"I didn't know what to say, because I suddenly sensed that he knew the truth about the show. I had thought of telling him, but I hadn't been able to.

"[He] urged me to 'wipe the slate clean, start over.'

" 'You think the slate is dirty?' I couldn't look at him.

"We walked along for a while. Then he said, 'It's none of my business. Dirty or not — and I don't know what "dirty" would be — the fact is you're caught up in something you may not really want.' That was as direct as he got that day. 'Sometimes I think you're having a lot of fun, other times you seem sad. I think turning your back on all of it might make you really happy.'

"Tears came. 'Dad,' I said, 'I'm sorry, but it's just not possible.'

" 'Why not possible?'

" 'I'm afraid there's no way out anymore. In a way . . . I think I'd like to have done what you describe. As far as fame is concerned, you know as well as I do that celebrity isn't the same as fame.' Finally, I said, 'Oh, shit, Dad, I wish I were . . . free to do this.' My father and I never talked about it again."[22]

Finally, he recounts a gift from his father, given after his congressional testimony.

"He had wrapped a square box in tissue paper, sealed with Scotch tape. The box contained a gyroscopic compass, the kind you can start spinning and put on the edge of a glass, where it will stay upright until the spinning stops. A card in the box read, 'May this be for you the whirligig of time that brings in his revenges.' I knew the quotation. It's from *Twelfth Night*. Feste, the mean-spirited clown, has been unmasked, but those are his last words, thrown over his shoulder. The play's audience knows that somehow he will survive and live to taunt some other master. I didn't ask my father what he had meant by it, because I knew he was saying that I, too, would survive and somehow find a way back. I just hugged him and said, 'Thank you, Papa.' "[23]

***

Twenty-One host **Jack Barry** died in 1984 at age 66.

Joseph Cates, producer of *The $64,000 Question*, died in 1998 at age 74.

Louis Cowan, producer-creator of *The $64,000 Question*, passed in 1976 at age 66.

Advertising executive **Walter Craig,** who helped bring *The $64,000 Question* to television, passed at age 85 in 2011.

Twenty-One producer **Dan Enright** died in 1992 at age 74.

Congressional investigator **Richard Goodwin** died in 2018 at age 86.

Whistleblower **Charles E. "Stoney" Jackson, Jr.** died in 2002 at age 88.

The $64,000 Question producer **Mert Koplin** passed in 1992 at age 71.

Hal March, host of *The $64,000 Question*, died in 1970 at age 49.

Charles Revson, head of Revlon from 1932 to 1975, passed in 1975 at age 68.

Twenty-One contestant and whistleblower **Herbert Stempel** passed away at 93 in 2020.

Manhattan Assistant District Attorney **Joseph Stone** passed in 2003.

Twenty-One contestant **Charles Van Doren** passed away at 93 in 2019.

ABOUT THE AUTHOR

David Inman grew up watching too much television. He parlayed that into a gig as the author of "The Incredible Inman," a nationally syndicated TV and movie trivia Q&A column that ran from 1981-2013. He has also supplied material for Turner Classic Movies hosts Ben Mankiewicz and Dave Karger, and he is the author of several books, including *Performers' Television Credits, 1948-2000* (McFarland, 2001); *Television Variety Shows* (McFarland, 2005); and *Louisville Television* (Arcadia Publishing, 2010). His other writing can be viewed at www.theincredibleinman.com and he can reached at incredibleinman@yahoo.com.

BIBLIOGRAPHY

Barnouw, Eric. *The Sponsor: Notes on Modern Potentates.* New York: Routledge, 2017.

Fabe, Maxene. *TV Game Shows.* New York: Doubleday, 1979.

Fox, Stephen. *The Mirror Makers: A History of American Advertising and Its Creators.* Champaign: University of Illinois Press, 1997.

Friendly, Fred. *Due to Circumstances Beyond Our Control ....* New York: Vintage Books, 1968.

Fuller-Seeley, Kathryn H. *Jack Benny and the Golden Age of Radio Comedy.* Oakland: University of California Press, 2017.

Goodwin, Richard N. *Remembering America: A Voice from the Sixties.* Boston: Little, Brown & Company, 1988.

Halberstam, David. *The Fifties.* New York: Villard Books, 1993.

Inman, David M. *Performers' Television Credits, 1948-2000.* Jefferson, NC: McFarland & Company, Inc., 2001.

Inman, David M. *Television Variety Shows.* Jefferson, NC: McFarland & Company, 2005.

Investigation of Television Quiz Shows. Hearings Before a Subcommittee of the Committee on Interstate and Foreign Commerce, House of Representatives, 86th Cong., First Session, parts 1 and 2. Washington, D.C.: U.S. Government Printing Office, 1960.

Kisseloff, Jeff. *The Box: An Oral History of Television, 1920-61.* New York: Viking Books, 1995.

Pease, Edward C. and Dennis, Everette E., Editors. *Radio — The Forgotten Medium.* London: Routledge, 2018.

Rudel, Anthony J. *Hello, Everybody! The Dawn of American Radio.* New York: Harcourt, Inc., 2008.

Sperber, Ann M. *Murrow: His Life and Times.* New York: Freundlich Books, 1986.

Stone, Joseph and Yohn, Timothy M. *Prime Time and Misdemeanors: Investigating the 1950s TV Quiz Scandal -- A D.A.'s Account.* New Brunswick, NJ: Rutgers University Press, 1992.

Tobias, Andrew. *Fire and Ice: The Story of Charles Revson -- The Man Who Built the Revlon Empire.* New York: William Morrow and Company, 1976.

FOOTNOTES

INTRODUCTION

1. https://www.encyclopedia.com/history/culture-magazines/1950s-tv-and-radio

2. Epstein, Florence. "After 18 Years, the Jackpot," *Screenland,* January 1956, p. 62.

3. *"The $64,000 Question,"* June 7, 1955. Viewed at The Paley Center for Media, New York, NY.

CHAPTER ONE: A SHORT HISTORY OF COMMERCIAL BROADCASTING — OR, THE SPONSOR, THE SPOT AND THE STUTTERING SHOWGIRL

1. Armstrong, Charlotte. "Mr. Sponsor Asks . . . ," *Sponsor,* September 25, 1950, p. 38.

2. Pease, Edward C. and Dennis, Everette E., Editors. *Radio — The Forgotten Medium.* London: Routledge, 2018.

3. Rudel, Anthony J. *Hello, Everybody! The Dawn of American Radio.* New York: Harcourt, Inc., 2008, p. 96.

4. " — But We've Got to Have It!" *Radio Stars,* April 1933, p. 41.

5. Barnouw, Eric. *The Sponsor: Notes on Modern Potentates.* New York: Routledge, 2017, p. 17.

6. Rudel, p. 231.

7. "Do They Earn Their Pay?" *Radio Stars,* July 1934, p. 14.

8. Rudel, p. 317.

9. Kisseloff, Jeff. *The Box: An Oral History of Television, 1920-61.* New York: Viking Books, 1995, p. 507.

10. *The Jell-O Program,* April 5, 1936. Accessed on YouTube: https://www.youtube.com/watch?v=hrKPxjo7b7c&list=PLq-LI3Yx R4OLi8MoAqaC-RQ1ZTJ3gI87M&index=20

11. *The Jell-O Program*, February 7, 1937. Accessed on YouTube: https://www.youtube.com/watch?v=yVaacHBKGjc&list= PL76MtjEzwZpykrC1AmyCp2UVlc3aFXuM8&index=6

12. Fuller-Seeley, Kathryn H. *Jack Benny and the Golden Age of Radio Comedy*. Oakland: University of California Press, 2017, p. 193.

13. Fuller-Seeley, p. 215.

14. http://www.old-time.com/commercials/1940%27s/Cigarette%20Pack%20Color.htm

15. "Lucky White," *Broadcasting*, November 16, 1942, p. 53; "Golenpaul Negotiates with Several Potentional [sic] Sponsors for *Information Please*," *Broadcasting*, December 21, 1942, p. 56.

16. "Monday Period on NBC Is Selected by Heinz for *Information Please*," *Broadcasting*, January 18, 1943, p. 18.

17. "Golenpaul Denied Jingle Injunction — *Information Please* Must Use Plug in Final Broadcasts," *Broadcasting*, February 1, 1943, p. 41.

18. http://adage.com/article/special-report-the-advertising-century/ad-age-advertising-century-timeline/143661/

19. "Television Reviews," *Variety*, September 6, 1939; p. 26.

20. https://en.wikipedia.org/wiki/Television_advertisement

21. Fox, Stephen. *The Mirror Makers: A History of American Advertising and Its Creators*. Champaign: University of Illinois Press, 1997, p. 178.

22. Millstein, Gilbert. "Its Creator Explains the *$64,000* Appeal," *The New York Times Magazine*, August 21, 1955, p. 30.

23. Ibid.

24. Halberstam, David. *The Fifties*. New York: Villard Books, 1993, p. 644.

25. *American Experience: The Quiz Show Scandals*, PBS, 1992. Accessed on YouTube: https://www.youtube.com/watch?v=hSCHLnMHd04&t=2741s. Also: https://www.pbs.org/wgbh/americanexperience/films/quizshow/#transcript

26. Ibid.

27. Tobias, Andrew. *Fire and Ice: The Story of Charles Revson — The Man Who Built the Revlon Empire.* New York: William Morrow and Company, 1976, p. 145.

28. "Agency Profile," *Sponsor,* August 22, 1955, p. 84.

29. Ibid.

30. http://adage.com/article/adage-encyclopedia/norman-craig-kummel/98801/

31. "TV Talk," *Modern Screen,* March 1956, p. 20.

32. "The $60 Million Question," *Time,* April 22, 1957, p. 78.

33. Tobias, p. 153.

34. Ibid, p. 156.

35. Kisseloff, p. 479.

36. Tobias, p. 23.

37. http://www.cosmeticsandskin.com/companies/hazel-bishop.php

38. Tobias, p. 146.

39. http://adage.com/article/special-report-the-advertising-century/ad-age-advertising-century-timeline/143661/

CHAPTER TWO: "THE PROGRAM WHERE KNOWLEDGE IS KING AND THE REWARD KING-SIZED"

1. "For Revlon, Money Has Become Water," *Billboard,* June 11, 1955, p. 7.

2. "Television Reviews," *Variety,* June 15, 1955, p. 31.

3. Ibid; Stahl, Bob. "A Summer Show Hits the Jackpot," *TV Guide,* August 20, 1955, p. 6.

4. Berger, Meyer. "About New York: A Patrolman Bones Up on the Bard," *The New York Times,* June 10, 1955, p. 27.

5. *American Experience: The Quiz Show Scandals,* PBS, 1992. Accessed on YouTube: https://www.youtube.com/watch?v=hSCHLnMHd04&t=2741s. Also: https://www.pbs.org/wgbh/americanexperience/films/quizshow/#transcript

6. Tobias, p. 146.

7. Kisseloff, p. 386.

8. "NBC-TV Sets *Big Surprise* as Gleason Problem Answer," *Billboard,* August 20, 1955, p. 1.

9. "Agency Profile," *Sponsor,* August 22, 1955, p. 84.

10. Stahl, Bob. "A Summer Show Hits the Jackpot," *TV Guide,* August 20, 1955, p. 5.

11. "*$64,000 Question's* Global Coverage," *Variety,* July 13, 1955, p. 28.

12. Stahl, Bob. "A Summer Show Hits the Jackpot," *TV Guide,* August 20, 1955, p. 4.

13. "$32,000 and Mother," *Broadcasting,* July 25, 1955, p. 86.

14. "Bible Bumps Baseball," *Variety,* July 13, 1955, p. 25.

15. "Tele Follow-Ups," *Variety,* July 20, 1955, p. 31.

16. "Bible-Totin' Grandma Gets Own Telepix Show," *Variety,* September 28, 1955, p. 1.

17. Bolstad, Helen. "Miracle in Music," *TV-Radio Mirror,* November 1955, p. 80.

18. Ibid.

19. "Radio and TV: Fort Knox or Bust?," *Time,* August 22, 1955, p. 47.

20. "Tuesday *Question* Clocks 30,000,000 TViewers; Show to Be Simulcast," *Daily Variety,* August 11, 1955, p. 14.

21. "Inside Stuff — Radio-TV," *Variety,* August 10, 1955, p. 34; "Opera Interest," *Broadcasting,* August 15, 1955, p. 7.

22. "Prato Wows 'Em in Pitt: *$64,000* Opera Expert Gets the Red Carpet Treatment During Four-Day Visit," *Variety,* November 2, 1955, p. 27.

23. Hellman, Jack. "Light and Airy," *Daily Variety,* August 11, 1955, p. 14.

24. http://www.cosmeticsandskin.com/cdc/question.php

25. Tobias, p. 146.

26. "She Leads Three Lives," *TV Guide,* December 17, 1955, p. 20.

27. Tobias, pp. 150-151.

28. "Sponsor-Scope," *Sponsor,* November 10, 1956, p. 11.

29. Tobias, p. 150-151.

30. "Gloria Lockerman Quits Quiz," *Jet,* September 15, 1955, p. 10.

31. https://uselessetymology.com/2024/03/08/how-12-year-old-gloria-lockerman-taught-us-the-word-disestablishmentarianism/

32. "*Mademoiselle's* Choices," *Variety,* December 21, 1955, p. 53.

33. "64G Goes Live on Coast-to-Coast Net," *Billboard,* September 24, 1955.

34. Shanley, J.P. "Marine Wins $64,000 TV Quiz; Aided by Father in Food Queries," *The New York Times,* September 14, 1955, p. 1.

35. "Capt. McCutcheon's 58,980,000 Viewers," *Variety,* October 5, 1955, p. 1.

36. Shanley, J.P. "Marine Wins $64,000 TV Quiz; Aided by Father in Food Queries," *The New York Times,* September 14, 1955, p. 1.

37. Kisseloff, p. 466.

38. Halberstam, p. 646.

39. Shanley, J.P. "Marine Wins $64,000 TV Quiz; Aided by Father in Food Queries," *The New York Times,* September 14, 1955, p. 71.

40. "*$64,000 Question* Menu for Hotel New Yorker," *Variety,* September 21, 1955, p. 2.

41. "Back in Working Clothes: Loretta Young Returns After Her Long Illness," *TV Guide,* January 14, 1956, p. 16.

42. Csida, Joe. "Sponsor Backstage: What the John Crosbys and Jack Goulds Contribute," *Sponsor,* October 3, 1955, p. 28.

43. "M & L Face Suit on *$64,000* Takeoff," *Variety,* September 14, 1955, p. 1.

44. "Tele Follow-Up Comment," *Variety,* October 12, 1955, p. 38.

45. "The Great Gold Rush — 'Come and Get It' Is the Network Cry in War of Giveaways," *TV Guide,* September 24, 1955, p. 12.

46. "Five $64,000,000 TV Questions." *Sponsor*, October 17, 1955, p. 117.

47. "Television Reviews," *Daily Variety*, October 10, 1955, p. 8.

48. Adams, Val. "Mrs. Power, Fan, Bats in $32,000," *The New York Times*, September 21, 1955, p. 67.

49. "NBC's Cuffo Daytime Spread Plus Half-Hour Nighttime to Revlon in *$64,000 Question* Power Play Bid," *Variety*, September 21, 1955, pp. 29 and 46.

50. Ibid.

51. Rosen, George. "There's Hardly a Man Alive Today Who Won't Remember the *$64,000* Raid That Hasn't Jelled," *Variety*, September 28, 1955. p. 27.

52. Rosen, George. "*$64,000* — TV's Top Whodunit: New Clues Put NBC in the Clear," *Variety*, October 5, 1955, pp. 23 and 46.

53. Tobias, p. 150.

54. "Revsons' Tale of 2 Quizzers Poses Agency Problem," *Variety*, December 7, 1955, p. 30.

55. "BBDO, LaRoche Get More Revlon Business," *Advertising Age*, January 16, 1956, p 1.

56. "Who Does What to Whom Next?," *Variety*, January 11, 1956, p. 29.

57. "Revlon Explodes a $3,500,000 *Big Surprise* at Agency, Gives Biz, *$64,000 Question* to BBD&O," *Variety*, January 11, 1956, p. 29.

CHAPTER THREE: "STIFF HIM"

1. "Revlon's '55 Sales Zoom 54% Over 1954," *Broadcasting*, January 30, 1956, p. 28.

2. https://cosmeticsandskin.com/companies/revlon-1945.php

3. "Why is *$64,000 Question* Liked?," *Sponsor*, December 26, 1955, p. 2.

4. Elliott, Stuart. "An Old Industry Name Signals a Shift Into a New Era," *The New York Times*, November 21, 2010, p B6.

5. Kisseloff, pp. 480-481.

6. *American Experience: The Quiz Show Scandals*, PBS, 1992. Accessed on YouTube: https://www.youtube.com/watch?v=h SCHLnMHd04&t=2741s. Also: https://www.pbs.org/wgbh/ americanexperience/films/quizshow/#transcript

7. Ibid.

8. Ibid.

9. "From the Production Centers . . . in San Francisco," *Variety*, December 14, 1955, p. 46.

10. "Dr. Joyce Brothers Set for Toronto Nitery Date New Year's at $1,000," *Variety*, December 21, 1955, p. 1.

11. Stone, Joseph and Yohn, Timothy M. *Prime Time and Misdemeanors: Investigating the 1950s TV Quiz Scandal — A D.A.'s Account.* New Brunswick, NJ: Rutgers University Press, 1992, p. 137.

12. "Cobbler Sews Up $64,000 Booty; To Stage Operas with Winnings," *The New York Times*, February 15, 1956, p. 67.

13. Fabe, Maxene. *TV Game Shows.* New York: Doubleday, 1979, p. 198.

14. Carter, Joan. "Old-Fashioned Love, Modern Style," *TV-Radio Mirror*, February 1956, p. 44.

15. "Quiz-Crazy Italy," *Variety*, March 28, 1956, p. 34.

16. "Television Reviews," *Variety*, April 11, 1956, p. 30.

17. "The Artful Jockey," *Newsweek*, April 30, 1956, p. 78.

18. "Highlights: '55-'56 Show Management Review — Special Citations." *Variety*, April 18, 1956, p. 29.

19. "Tele Follow-Up Comment," *Variety*, June 13, 1956, p. 35.

20. "Allen Cracks Top 10," *Variety*, July 18, 1956, p. 22.

21. "His Own Expert," *Newsweek*, July 16, 1956, p. 81.

22. "Those Quiz Shows Are a Hit — Anywhere," *TV Guide*, October 6, 1956, p. 26.

23. Ibid.

24. Carlin, Steve. "Those *$64,000 Question* Rumors — The Producer Answers Some Nasty Whispers," *TV Guide*, September 22, 1956, p. 4.

25. "Benny on *64G*," *Variety*, October 2, 1957, p. 39; Green, Abel. "Don't Rewrite a Hit," *Variety*, October 16, 1957, p. 35.

26. "Jackie Coogan Picks Silent Pix as Category in *64G Challenge* Bid," *Variety*, January 30, 1957, p. 26.

27. "TV's Round-Robin of Plugolas Highlighted by Robinson and Logan," *Variety*, September 26, 1956, p. 29.

28. "*Can Do* Subs *Beautiful Girl*," *Variety*, November 14, 1956, p. 28.

29. *American Experience: The Quiz Show Scandals*, PBS, 1992. Accessed on YouTube: https://www.youtube.com/watch?v=hSCHLnMHd04&t=2741s. Also: https://www.pbs.org/wgbh/americanexperience/films/quizshow/#transcript

30. Ibid.

31. *Twenty-One*, November 14, 1956. Viewed at The Paley Center for Media, New York, NY.

32. *American Experience: The Quiz Show Scandals*, PBS, 1992. Accessed on YouTube: https://www.youtube.com/watch?v=hSCHLnMHd04&t=2741s. Also; https://www.pbs.org/wgbh/americanexperience/films/quizshow/#transcript

33. Ibid.

34. Ibid.

35. Ibid.

36. Stone, p. 318; "Federal Trade Commission Eyeing Contestant Rules of TV *Big Surprise*," *Variety*, January 16, 1957, p. 1.

37. Stone, p. 148.

38. "High Tension on *21*," *TV-Radio Mirror*, June 1957, p. 20.

39. Levy, Alan. "Aftermath of a Scandal," *Redbook*, November 1961, p. 129.

40. Halberstam, p. 653.

41. *American Experience: The Quiz Show Scandals*, PBS, 1992. Accessed on YouTube: https://www.youtube.com/watch?v=hSCHLnMHd04&t=2741s. Also: https://www.pbs.org/wgbh/americanexperience/films/quizshow/#transcript

42. "Of Time and TV," *Variety*, February 20, 1957, p. 23.

43. Stahl, Bob. "A Dillar, a Dollar — A 9 O'Clock Scholar Tells How It Feels to Win a Fortune," *TV Guide*, February 23, 1957, p. 6.

44. *American Experience: The Quiz Show Scandals*, PBS, 1992. Accessed on YouTube: https://www.youtube.com/watch?v=hSCHLnMHd04&t=2741s. Also: https://www.pbs.org/wgbh/americanexperience/films/quizshow/#transcript

45. "Van Doren Goes Out in a Blaze of Glory as *21* Trounces *Lucy*," *Variety*, March 13, 1957, p. 23.

46. "TV Talk," *Modern Screen*, June 1957, p. 14.

47. "Van Doren Dethroned on TV Quiz by a Woman Who Knows Kings," *The New York Times*, March 12, 1957, p. 67.

48. "Making Money by Giving It Away," *Broadcasting*, March 18, 1957, p. 27.

49. "Uplifting Brought Down to Earth," *Broadcasting*, March 4, 1957, p. 69.

50. "Return of Van Doren — Astride NBC Contract," *Broadcasting*, April 15, 1957, p. 41.

CHAPTER FOUR: "IT WAS A CON GAME, THAT'S ALL"

1. Hall, Gladys. "What *THE $64,000 Question* Meant to Me," *TV-Radio Mirror*, March 1957, p. 32.

2. "1956 Nielsen Rating Leaders," *Sponsor*, February 9, 1957, p. 56.

3. "Making Money by Giving It Away," *Broadcasting*, March 18, 1957, p. 28.

4. "TV Quiz Shows Start Feuding; Battle of the Van Doren *Challenge*," *Variety*, February 13, 1957, p. 1.

5. Hellman, Jack. "Light and Airy," *Daily Variety,* April 11, 1957, p. 16.

6. DeBlois, Frank. "Fantabulous 10-Year-Old — An Evening with Robert Strom, Whose Knowledge Has Astounded the Nation," *TV Guide,* May 4, 1957, p. 9.

7. Hellman, Jack. "Light and Airy," *Daily Variety,* June 27, 1957, p. 10.

8. Academy of American Television interview with Barbara Feldon. Accessed on YouTube: https://www.youtube.com/watch?v=pDK2AxO5CTI&t=266s

9. Hall, Gladys. "What *THE $64,000 Question* Meant to Me," *TV-Radio Mirror,* March 1957, p. 34.

10. "Quiz Complications — Nigerian Bible Expert Quits *The 64,000 Question* for Matrimonial Reasons," *The New York Times,* December 18. 1957, p. 71.

11. "The $60 Million Question," *Time,* April 22, 1957, p. 78.

12. *American Experience: The Quiz Show Scandals,* PBS, 1992. Accessed on YouTube: https://www.youtube.com/watch?v=hSCHLnMHd04&t=2741s. Also: https://www.pbs.org/wgbh/americanexperience/films/quizshow/#transcript

13. Herbert Stempel obituary, *The Denver Post,* May 31, 2020: https://www.denverpost.com/2020/05/31/herbert-stempel-dies/

14. "NBC Buys Out Barry & Enright," *Variety,* March 20, 1957, p. 23.

15. *American Experience: The Quiz Show Scandals,* PBS, 1992. Accessed on YouTube: https://www.youtube.com/watch?v=hSCHLnMHd04&t=2741s. Also: https://www.pbs.org/wgbh/americanexperience/films/quizshow/#transcript

16. Rosenberg, Howard. "How Did the '50s Quiz Show Scandal Ensnare a Tennessee Minister?," *The Los Angeles Times,* November 5, 1989.

17. Ibid.

18. DeBlois, Frank. "The Morning After — Al Einfrank Tells How It Feels to Lose $64,000," *TV Guide*, February 23, 1957, p. 8; "So Ends An Era of Cadillac Giveaways," *Broadcasting*, November 10, 1958, p. 50.

19. Aldrich, David. "Are Quiz Shows Fixed?," *Look*, August 20, 1957, p. 45.

20. *American Experience: The Quiz Show Scandals*, PBS, 1992. Accessed on YouTube: https://www.youtube.com/watch?v=hSCHLnMHd04&t=2741s. Also: https://www.pbs.org/wgbh/americanexperience/films/quizshow/#transcript

21. Rosenberg.

22. "*64G Challenge*, Clients at Odds on Retaining Show," *Variety*, January 15, 1958, p. 32.

23. "NBC's No. 1 Status on ARB's Top 25 for Feb.; CBS Commands Top 10," *Variety*, March 5, 1958, p. 28.

24. "Cowan Named CBS-TV Prexy," *Variety*, March 12, 1958, p. 25.

25. Csida, Joe. "Where Did Martin Go?," *Sponsor*, June 28, 1958, p. 18.

26. Kisseloff, p. 480.

27. "A Family Affair," *Time*, March 28, 1960, p. 97.

28. "The Unflabbergasted Genius," *Time*, November 16, 1959, p. 106.

29. "The Quizzes," *Broadcasting*, August 4, 1958, p. 14.

CHAPTER FIVE: "THESE QUIZ SHOWS ARE DRIVING US CRAZY"

1. Stone, p. 15.

2. Stone, p. 24.

3. Stone, p. 77.

4. Adams, Val. "Quiz Show Replaced," *The New York Times*, August 19, 1958, p. 55.

5. "*Dotto* Gives Away the Game, So Colgate Gives It the Gate on Both Networks; Affidavit Sent to FCC," *Variety*, August 20, 1958, p. 23.

6. Kleiner, Dick. "*Dotto* Case Casts Shadow on Quiz," NEA Syndicate, August 20, 1958.

7. Torre, Marie. "Television Today: He Did It and He's Glad," *The Cedar Rapids Gazette*, September 3, 1959, p. 8.

8. Van Horne, Harriet. "How *Dotto* Quiz Got TV's Axe," Scripps-Howard Syndicate, August 27, 1958.

9. "*Dotto* Pyramids Jackpot Headache in TV Quizzical Sweepstakes," *Variety*, August 27, 1958, pp. 1 and 42.

10. *American Experience: The Quiz Show Scandals*, PBS, 1992. Accessed on YouTube: https://www.youtube.com/watch?v=hSCHLnMHd04&t=2741s. Also: https://www.pbs.org/wgbh/americanexperience/films/quizshow/#transcript

11. Ibid.

12. "TV Quiz Business Is Itself Quizzed About Fix Charges," *Life*, September 15, 1958, p. 23.

13. "Producers Offer Documents Refuting Charges That *Twenty-One* Was Rigged," *Broadcasting*, September 1, 1958, p. 9.

14. Adams, Val. "Record Is Played on TV 'Blackmail' — *21* Producers Offer Taped Conversation to Support Their Extortion Charge," *The New York Times*, September 3, 1958, p. 67.

15. *American Experience: The Quiz Show Scandals*, PBS, 1992. Accessed on YouTube: https://www.youtube.com/watch?v=hSCHLnMHd04&t=2741s. Also: https://www.pbs.org/wgbh/americanexperience/films/quizshow/#transcript

16. "Quiz Furor Heading for N.Y. Grand Jury," *Broadcasting*. September 15, 1958, p. 40.

17. Shanley, John P. "A *Dotto* Winner Says She Got Aid," *The New York Times*, September 6, 1958, p. 29.

18. Adams, Val. "TV-Quiz Inquiry Widened in City," *The New York Times*, August 28, 1958, p. 29.

19. "Minister Says Quiz Gave Him TV Reply," *The New York Times,* September 7, 1958, p. 86.

20. "Cig Firm Dropping *$64,000 Challenge,*" *Daily Variety,* September 15, 1958, pp. 1 and 7.

21. "Tender Trap," *Sponsor,* September 27, 1958, p. 30.

22. Adams, Val. "NBC to Present News Show in Place of *$64,000 Challenge,*" *The New York Times,* September 15, 1958, p. 40.

23. "Tele Follow-Up Comment," *Variety,* September 3, 1958, p. 24.

24. "Hope's Socko 1-Liners," *Variety,* September 17, 1958, p. 35.

25. "The Week of the Quizlings," *Variety,* September 3, 1958, p. 38.

26. "Ollie Treyz: 'The Only Fixed Shows We Have on ABC Are the Westerns,' " *Variety,* September 24, 1958, p. 20.

27. "TV Quiz Business Is Itself Quizzed About Fix Charges," *Life,* September 15, 1958, p. 22.

28. "Cates: Quiz Shows Were Already Waning, Current Hubbub Only Greased the Skids," *Broadcasting,* September 29, 1958, p. 48.

29. Stone, pp. 55-56.

30. Stone, p. 58.

31. Stone, p. 5.

32. Stone, p. 63.

33. Stone, pp. 68-69.

34. Stone, p. 102.

35. Stone, p. 83.

36. Stone, p. 101.

37. "*Twenty-One* Producer Indicted," *Broadcasting,* November 10, 1958, p. 9.

38. Stone, p. 134.

39. Adams, Val. "News of TV and Radio: Hot Half Hour," *The New York Times,* September 7, 1958, p. X-15.

40. "NBC Takes on Production of Barry-Enright Quizzes," *Broadcasting.* October 6, 1958, p. 9.

41. "Barry and Enright Relinquish Production of TV Quizzers," *Variety,* October 8, 1958, p. 24.

42. "Fun with a Trendex," *Variety*, October 8, 1958, p. 25.

43. Rosen, George. "New TV Season in Rut Race," *Variety*, October 15, 1958, p. 52.

44. "*21* Dropped, *Question* Hitting Skids on Ratings," *Broadcasting*, October 20, 1958, p. 76.

45. "So Ends an Era of Cadillac Giveaways," *Broadcasting*, November 10, 1958, p. 50.

46. Stone, pp. 139-140.

47. Stone, p. 141.

48. Stone, p. 139.

49. Stone, p. 183.

50. Stone, p. 145.

51. Stone, p. 150.

52. "A Sad Ending to the Quiz Era," *Broadcasting*, November 9, 1959, p. 44.

53. Stone, p. 183.

54. Stone, p. 170.

55. Stone, p. 160.

56. Stone, p. 171.

57. Stone, p. 197.

58. Stone, p. 198.

59. Stone, p. 197.

60. Stone, p. 200.

61. Ibid.

62. Stone, p. 201.

63. Ibid.

CHAPTER SIX: "WE PLAYED THE WHOLE THING LIKE A SOLEMN MINUET"

1. Congressional testimony, p. 323.

2. Stone, p. 207.

3. Ibid.

4. Goodwin, Richard N. *Remembering America: A Voice from the Sixties.* Boston: Little, Brown & Company, 1988, p. 42.

5. Goodwin, p. 43.

6. "Congress Quizzing on TV Quizzes," *Broadcasting,* August 3. 1959, p. 38.

7. Goodwin, p. 46.

8. Stone, p. 211.

9. Kisseloff, p. 494-495.

10. Stone, pp. 212-213.

11. Goodwin, p. 48.

12. Goodwin, p. 49.

13. Goodwin, p. 55.

14. "House Fans TV Quiz Ashes to Life," *Broadcasting.* October 12, 1959, p. 78.

15. Stone, p. 220.

16. "House Fans TV Quiz Ashes to Life," *Broadcasting.* October 12, 1959, p. 79.

17. Congressional testimony, p. 51.

18. Congressional testimony, p. 55.

19. "House Fans TV Quiz Ashes to Life," *Broadcasting.* October 12, 1959, p. 82.

20. Congressional testimony, p. 63.

21. Congressional testimony, p. 72.

22. Blair, William M. "Two Testify *21* Quiz Was Fixed," *The New York Times,* October 7, 1959, p. 47.

23. Congressional testimony, p. 103.

24. Congressional testimony, p. 104.

25. Congressional testimony, p. 136.

26. Congressional testimony, pp. 151-152.

27. Congressional testimony, p. 114.

28. "House Fans TV Quiz Ashes to Life," *Broadcasting.* October 12, 1959, p. 87.

29. Congressional testimony, p. 129.

30. "House Fans TV Quiz Ashes to Life," *Broadcasting.* October 12, 1959, p. 87.

31. Congressional testimony, p. 157.

32. Congressional testimony, pp. 161-162.

33. Congressional testimony, p. 171.

34. "House Fans TV Quiz Ashes to Life," *Broadcasting.* October 12, 1959, p. 84.

35. Blair, William M. "Van Doren Taken Off Air by NBC in TV Quiz Inquiry," *The New York Times,* October 9. 1959, p. 1.

36. Stone, p. 72.

37. Blair, William M. "Van Doren Taken Off Air by NBC in TV Quiz Inquiry," *The New York Times,* October 9. 1959, p. 1.

38. "Crackdown on TV Programs?," *Broadcasting.* October 12, 1959, p. 28.

39. Ibid.

40. Congressional testimony, p. 343.

41. "Crackdown on TV Programs?," *Broadcasting.* October 12, 1959, p. 28.

42. Blair, William M. "Enright Concedes Fixing TV Quizzes for 'Many Years,' " *The New York Times,* October 10, 1959, p. 1.

43. Congressional testimony, p. 252.

44. Congressional testimony, p. 216.

45. Congressional testimony, p. 315.

46. Stone, p. 226.

47. Congressional testimony, p. 326.

48. Congressional testimony, p. 335.

49. Goodwin, p. 56.

50. Kisseloff, p. 495.

51. Congressional testimony, p. 365.

52. Congressional testimony, p. 386.

53. Congressional testimony, p. 387.

54. Congressional testimony, pp. 392-393.

55. Congressional testimony, p. 406.

56. Congressional testimony, p. 458.

CHAPTER SEVEN: "I WAS INVOLVED, DEEPLY INVOLVED, IN A DECEPTION"

1. Baker, Russell. "Producer Describes Vexations in 'Subtly' Rigging Quiz Show — Says He Spurned Coaching Contestants in Favor of Using 'Existential Matrix' Method at Risk of Sponsor's Ire," *The New York Times*, November 4, 1958, p. 28.
2. "Quiz Hearing Spotlight Dimmed: Van Doren to Co-Star with *$64,000 Question* When Show Resumes." *Broadcasting.* October 19, 1959, p. 82.
3. Stone, p. 240.
4. "CBS, NBC Cite Quiz Housecleaning," *Broadcasting*, November 9, 1959, p. 33.
5. Stone, p. 241.
6. Stone, p. 245.
7. Stone, p. 246.
8. Stone, p. 247.
9. Stone, pp. 247-248.
10. "I Was Involved in a Deception," *Time*, November 16, 1959, p. 73.
11. Ibid.
12. Stone, p. 250.
13. Stone, p. 250.
14. Stone, p. 251.
15. "A Sad Ending to the Quiz Era," *Broadcasting*, November 9, 1959, p. 40.
16. "Editorial Comment," *New York Post*, November 3, 1959, p. A-26.
17. Lewis, Fulton Jr. "Van Doren Enmeshed by Lies," King Features Syndicate, November 3, 1959.
18. Kilgallen, Dorothy. "Hindsight on Charles Van Doren," King Features Syndicate. November 5, 1959.

19. "Hardly a Scratch in TV's Image," *Broadcasting*, November 2, 1959, p. 41.

20. "Now a Deep Scar in TV's Image," *Broadcasting*, November 9, 1959, p. 37.

21. Blair, William M. "Van Doren Admits Lying, Says TV Quiz Was Fixed; Loses His Columbia Post," *The New York Times*, November 3. 1959, p. 20.

22. Halberstam, p. 664.

23. "A Sad Ending to the Quiz Era," *Broadcasting*, November 9, 1959, p. 44.

24. "How It Was Done," *Time*, November 16, 1959, p. 74.

25. Congressional testimony, pp. 661-662.

26. "A Sad Ending to the Quiz Era," *Broadcasting*, November 9, 1959, p. 42.

27. "A Sad Ending to the Quiz Era," *Broadcasting*, November 9, 1959, p. 44.

28. "A Sad Ending to the Quiz Era," *Broadcasting*, November 9, 1959, p. 48.

29. Stone, p. 257.

30. "CBS, NBC Cite Quiz Housecleaning: Abrams Testimony," *Broadcasting*, November 9, 1959, p. 33.

31. "At Liberty," *Broadcasting*, November 9, 1959, p. 48.

32. Stone, p. 258.

33. "A Sad Ending to the Quiz Era," *Broadcasting*, November 9, 1959, p. 48.

34. Ibid.

35. "The Unflabbergasted Genius," *Time*, November 16, 1959, p. 106.

36. Stone, p. 260.

37. Stone, p. 261.

38. "A Sad Ending to the Quiz Era," *Broadcasting*, November 9, 1959, pp. 53-54.

39. "The Ultimate Responsibility," *Time*, November 16, 1959, p. 74.

40. "$30,000 Reported Paid to 'Plug' Safes on TV," *The New York Times*, November 15, 1959, p. 84.

41. "The Ultimate Responsibility," *Time*, November 16, 1959, p. 74.

42. Ibid.

43. Stone, p. 268.

44. Kisseloff, p. 497.

45. Goodwin, p. 62.

46. Ibid.

47. "The Tarnished Image," *Time*, November 16, 1959, p. 72.

48. "The Ultimate Responsibility," *Time*, November 16, 1959, p. 74.

49. "Letters," *TV Guide*, November 21, 1959, p. A-2.

50. "Hal March Asserts He Will Sue Revlon," Associated Press, November 4, 1959.

51. Morse, Jim. "Hal March Happy to Be Back on the Stage," North American Newspaper Alliance, August 19, 1959.

52. "How It Was Done," *Time*, November 16, 1959, p. 74.

53. "Many Quiz Show Victors Insist They Won Contests Without Fix," *The New York Times*, November 4, 1959, p. 28.

54. Stone, p. 275.

55. Stone, p. 323.

56. Stone, p. 306.

57. Stone, p. 303.

58. Stone, p. 309.

CHAPTER EIGHT: AFTERMATH

1. Levy, Alan. "Aftermath of a Scandal," *Redbook*, November 1961, p. 43.

2. Levy, Alan. "Aftermath of a Scandal," *Redbook*, November 1961, p. 126.

3. Friendly, Fred. *Due to Circumstances Beyond Our Control ....* New York: Vintage Books, 1968, p. 72.

4. Roth, Philip. *Zuckerman Unbound.* New York: Farrar, Straus & Giroux, 1981, pp. 17-20.

5. Van Doren 1985 *Today* appearance, accessed on YouTube; link has disappeared.

6. Halberstam, p. 666.

7. Van Doren, Charles. "All the Answers," *The New Yorker,* July 28, 2008, p. 69.

8. Redford interview with Bobbie Wygant, accessed on YouTube: https://www.youtube.com/watch?v=huiuWL2qlZk&t=460s

9. Kaufmann, Joanne. "Picks & Pans: Screen," *People,* September 19, 1994, p. 23.

10. Byrge, Duane. "Film Review: *Quiz Show,*" *The Hollywood Reporter,* p. 10.

11. Cerio, Gregory; Kahn, Toby; McFarland, Sabrina; and Longley, Anne. "The Answer Men: *Quiz Show* Evokes Haunting Memories for Three Figures from the '50s TV Scandal," *People,* October 3, 1994, p. 86.

12. Douthat, Strat. "Release of *Quiz Show* Puts Spotlight on Van Doren," Associated Press, October 2, 1994.

13. Cerio, Gregory; Kahn, Toby; McFarland, Sabrina; and Longley, Anne. "The Answer Men: *Quiz Show* Evokes Haunting Memories for Three Figures from the '50s TV Scandal," *People,* October 3, 1994, p. 88.

14. "To Be *Twenty-One* Again," *The Hollywood Reporter,* October 6, 1994, p. 6.

15. Herbert Stempel obituary, *The Denver Post,* May 31, 2020: https://www.denverpost.com/2020/05/31/herbert-stempel-dies/

16. Elliott, Stuart. "Geritol Sees Critical Film as a Potential Pick-Me-Up," *The New York Times,* September 22, 1994, p. 81.

17. Ibid.

18. Grove, Martin A. "Hollywood Report: Enright's Son Offers *Quiz Show* Disclaimer," *The Hollywood Reporter,* September 21, 1994, p. 8.

19. Carter, Bill. "Game Show Wins Regis," *The New York Times*, August 11, 1999, p. 9.

20. Van Doren, Charles. "All the Answers," *The New Yorker*, July 28, 2008, p. 69.

21. Ibid.

22. Van Doren, Charles. "All the Answers," *The New Yorker*, July 28, 2008, p. 65.

23. Van Doren, Charles. "All the Answers," *The New Yorker*, July 28, 2008, pp. 67-68.

INDEX